Lettuce in Your Kitchen

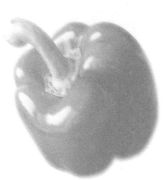

OTHER BOOKS BY
CHRIS SCHLESINGER
AND
JOHN WILLOUGHBY

....

THE THRILL OF
THE GRILL
Techniques, Recipes,
& Down-Home Barbecue

SALSAS, SAMBALS,
CHUTNEYS &
CHOWCHOWS
Intensely Flavored
"Little Dishes" from
Around the World

BIG FLAVORS
OF THE
HOT SUN
Hot Recipes and
Cool Tips from
the Spice Zone

Lettuce in Your Kitchen

WHERE SALAD GETS A WHOLE NEW SPIN AND DRESSINGS DO DOUBLE DUTY

CHRIS SCHLESINGER AND JOHN WILLOUGHBY

PHOTOGRAPHS BY CHRISTOPHER HIRSHEIMER

WILLIAM MORROW AND COMPANY, INC.
NEW YORK

Library of Congress Cataloging-in-Publication Data

Schlesinger, Chris.
    Lettuce in your kitchen: Where salad gets a whole new spin and dressings do double duty / Chris Schlesinger and John Willoughby; photographs by Christopher Hirsheimer. — 1st ed.
        p.   cm.
    Includes index.
    1. Salads. 2. Salad dressing. 3. Salad greens. I. Willoughby, John.   II. Title.
    TX740.S3245   1996
    641.8'3—dc20   95-46765
                                                            CIP

Printed in the United States of America
First Edition
1 2 3 4 5 6 7 8 9 10

BOOK DESIGN BY DON MORRIS DESIGN

Acknowledgments

Thanks to our editors: to Harriet Bell,

for her ready laugh, her keen eye

and ear, and her consistent attention

to the book and to Ann Bramson

for her grace, humor, and insight in

the final stages; to Doug Bellow

for his astute comments and his will-

ingness to wash, dry, and measure

untold quantities of greens; to our

agent, Doe Coover, for always

being in our corner; and to

Christopher Hirsheimer, for making

our food come to life in gorgeous

photography with the greatest of ease

and a fine sense of humor.

CONTENTS

v
Acknowledgments

I
Introduction

12
1 How to Use This Book

26
2 Ingredients: A Guide to Greens and Other Things

44
3 Simple Salads

78
4 Salads for the Perfect Tomato

94
5 Vegetable Salads

128
6 Salads with Meat and Fish

156
7 Main-Course Salads

184
8 Salads with Exotic Flavors

214
9 Fancy Salads

238
10 Salads for a Crowd

256
Index

INTRODUCTION

HOW DO YOU MAKE A SALAD? There's no rocket science involved. Just get your hands on some crisp, fresh greens; add a few other well-chosen ingredients; and toss with a flavor-packed dressing. That's the ball game.

That casual simplicity is one of the reasons why I have always loved salads. The other is that they just plain taste good. When I was growing up, there was always a salad on the family table. My mom put in whatever greens and vegetables she had around, and I loved the vinegary taste of her dressings. To me, salads were always a kind of interesting and variable vegetable course.

These days, when I go into a restaurant I am still likely to take the salad option, and when I'm cooking at home I will very often be making some kind of salad. Why? Because they are healthful, tasty, easy to make, and the dressings are fun to fool around with—an essential characteristic of any food that I truly enjoy.

While they're easy to make, though, salads are not so easy to define. They are so amenable to your mood or taste of the moment that they're hard to pin down. They can't be characterized by their place within the meal, for example, because a salad can be an appetizer, an entree, a side dish, or a healthful snack. They can't be defined by level of sophistication, either, because a salad can be a big, impressive production or an inventive, last-minute combination of whatever you have on hand. As for ingredients, a salad can be just some greens with dressing or can include anything from chicken to squid to mangoes.

So what exactly is a salad? To me, it is basically any dish that contains a high proportion of fresh, uncooked greens. This includes not only the traditional "salad greens" like lettuces and spinach but also spicy greens such as watercress or arugula; very young, tender versions of cooking greens such as beet, turnip, mustard, or kale; the wide family of Asian greens; cabbages; and even herbs like parsley or basil when used as whole leaves. My only qualification is that a salad include some kind of leafy green that is tender enough to eat without cooking.

Like most culinary definitions, this one is partly personal and partly historical. I go with this definition because I happen to really like greens and because I like feeling connected to the tradition of salads—a long and noble lineage that stretches at least as far back as written history.

Lettuce was eaten by the ancient Egyptians and it appears in tomb drawings at least 4,500 years old. Several varieties of lettuces, along with numerous other greens, were also a regular part of the diet of the ancient Greeks and Romans. In fact, the word *salad* can be traced back to the day when some nameless Roman epicure sprinkled salt over a head of romaine lettuce and dubbed it *herba salata*, or "salted greens." Over the centuries, this term has expanded so much that it now includes many dishes that bear little resemblance to that primal leafy snack. But to me these dishes—potato salad, pasta salad, shrimp salad, and so on—may be delicious, but they aren't really salads. My salads have got to include some of those greens.

The Romans quickly progressed from just salting their greens to dressing them with mixtures very similar to the vinaigrettes of today—simple combinations of olive oil, vinegar, and salt. Other ingredients—such as wine, honey, and the fermented fish sauce known as *garum*—soon appeared in the dressings, too.

Like some modern gourmands, a few of the ancients went overboard in their pursuit of salad pleasures, taking the idea a little more seriously than food deserves to be taken. The Greek philosopher Aristoxenus, for example, was said to be so obsessed with freshness that he would go out and sprinkle the lettuce in his garden with vinegar and honey the night before he planned to eat it, so it could be picked and eaten directly from the ground the next day. History doesn't record, though, how his early-morning salads tasted or whether the lettuce was consumed during the night by delighted ants.

In any case, most salad devotees took a more sensible approach to the dish, and the custom of eating greens with dressing continued to gain popularity right into the Middle Ages. A salad prepared by the English chefs who cooked for King Richard II toward the end of the fourteenth century, for example, included a whole array of greens—parsley, sage, borage, mint, maiden's leek, cress, fennel, rue, and purslane—tossed together with garlic, chives, onions, and leeks in a dressing of oil, vinegar, and salt.

Early Americans also seem to have enjoyed all kinds of greens. Thomas Jefferson mentions, for instance, that the common markets of his day could supply the cook not only with a variety of lettuce but also endive, sorrel, corn salad (mâche), and cress.

Somewhere along the line, though, we Americans seem to have temporarily lost our taste for greens. In the flush of modernism that followed World War II, we were seduced by canned and packaged foods, and we began looking more for convenience than for flavor. By the mid-twentieth century, to most people the word *salad* had come to mean not the flavorful mix of wild and cultivated greens that might have appeared on Jefferson's table but a wedge of iceberg lettuce accompanied by a couple of hard tomato quarters and some cucumber slices. Spinach or leaf lettuce might occasionally make its way into the salad bowls of more adventuresome eaters, but that was about it.

At the same time, salads began to be pigeonholed as a kind of culinary afterthought—something to be made with the left hand while the right hand was attending to the more "important" part of the meal. Even worse, salads began to be thought of as "diet food," a bland culinary mortification designed for weight loss rather than pleasure.

Fortunately, in the past decade greens have reentered our culinary consciousness. In some ways, this greens revival is simply part of a general rediscovery of the joys of real, deep flavors found in fresh, seasonal produce. The resurgence of interest in greens has also been helped immeasurably by improved transportation, which has made it possible to bring greens from the countryside to the city in large quantities while they are still relatively fresh.

But our new appreciation of greens also represents a victory over culinary closed-mindedness. After all, the difference between a green and a weed is often in the eye of the beholder. Dandelions, for example, were nothing but pests messing up the neat lawns where I grew up, and yellow-flowered mustard was a similar nuisance in meadows where cows grazed. I was astonished when I learned years later that people actually ate the leaves of both of these plants. Similarly, to most Americans, many of the world's finest greens used to be little more than marginally edible weeds, mysterious ingredients perhaps best left that way.

No longer. Today, greens of all varieties are increasingly available in produce stands and supermarkets around the country, with new ones showing up every day. As people across the country are more willing to try new products, to experiment with dishes and ingredients that they may not have had for dinner every night while growing up, their eyes have been opened to the many virtues of greens.

In the recipes in this book, I have tried to take advantage of the greens that are relatively new to us, as well as the ones that we know well. So while many of these recipes make use of familiar greens like iceberg, romaine, or Boston lettuce, others depend on varieties like arugula, radicchio, or dandelion greens, which have long been staples of Mediterranean cuisines but have only recently made their way to our supermarkets. And some recipes include even more recent additions to our national larder, like the many bitter-edged greens of Asia.

But whatever greens are used in a given recipe, you should always feel free to substitute and adapt to suit your own taste and what is available. After all, one of the great things about salads is that they are easygoing and flexible. What I have tried to do in this book is give you a lot of different ways to make salads, from simple to complicated, from straightforward to exotic. But to get back to basics, what you should never lose sight of is that salads have the three primary characteristics we always look for in food: they taste great, they're easy, and they're good for you.

The Health Factor

To me, the most important thing about greens is that they have fantastic intrinsic flavor. But as an added bonus, these leafy guys are also very good for you. Sometimes life just works out that way.

Lettuce and other greens of all sorts have traditionally been a staple part of the diet of the poor. This makes sense because greens were cheap: they could either be gathered wild from the field or grown in relatively large quantities even in small plots. Now we are finding that, like the grains and legumes that were also central to the diets of most of the world's people, greens are very healthful.

Greens are universally high in beneficial fiber. They also contain large amounts of vitamins C and E and beta-carotene, which are antioxidants that appear to help prevent cancer. In addition, the darker greens such as spinach, chard, kale, beet greens, mustard greens, bok choy, and mizuna contain significant amounts of folic acid, which helps prevent certain birth defects and may also assist in preventing some cancers. Most greens also contain high amounts of essential minerals, particularly iron and calcium, and some, such as dandelion greens and the cresses, have significant amounts of potassium.

But that covers only the more traditional nutritional field. Greens of all types are also rife with phytochemicals, the micronutrients that are coming to the fore in the field of diet and disease prevention. These micronutrients have names like indoles, isothiocyanates, and thiocyanates, which sound like nonsense terms to everyone but specialists in the field, but they are thought to be as important as beta-carotene in cancer prevention. Since scientists have not yet figured out which of these substances are responsible for what preventive function, the best we can do is follow the advice we have all heard from our mothers: "Eat your leafy greens."

1
HOW TO USE THIS BOOK

The #1 Rule: There Are No Rules

IN KEEPING WITH THE EASYGOING, informal nature of salads, there is no need to worry if one of the ingredients called for in a recipe can't be found, either in the pantry or at the farm stand down the road. It is perfectly acceptable to simply leave out the missing component or substitute something else that is available. Spinach Salad with Grilled Shrimp and Pineapple (page 154) is just fine without the shrimp, for example, or grilled scallops or bluefish can fill in for the absent crustacean.

In fact, you should feel free to eliminate just about any single ingredient if you are in a hurry, don't want such a substantial salad, or simply don't like the ingredient in question. For example, the salad of Baby Asian Greens with Ginger-Rubbed Chicken and Apricots (page 246) is easily transformed into a simple salad of baby Asian greens with gingery lemongrass dressing. The dressing and these wonderful, bittery greens still provide enough flavor punch to make an excellent salad.

In the same way, the easy adaptability of salads makes them a natural home for leftovers. If some grilled chicken from last night is sitting in the refrigerator, it can easily be substituted for fresh-grilled chicken breasts; likewise, leftover grilled steak makes a fine surrogate for lamb in the Salad of Arugula, Grilled Lamb, and Lima Beans (page 134).

Dealing with Greens

No matter which greens you use in your salad, there are certain things they have in common, including the fact that it pays off to take some care in choosing, cleaning, drying, and storing them.

CHOOSING GREENS The rules for choosing salad greens in the store are pretty much just common sense: like any other produce, you want to buy the greens that look freshest. That means that the leaves and stems should be crisp and free of brown spots. If possible, buy greens with roots still attached. The reason for this is that cutting off the roots exposes the ends of the greens to oxygen and starts the process of oxidation, which slowly leaches the nutrients and flavor from the greens.

Like a bad apple in a barrel, a bruised or wilted leaf or stem will promote decay among its neighboring greens. To prevent this, look the greens over as soon as you get them home, and remove any leaves that are wilted or show signs of decay. If there is a band holding the head or bunch together, take it off before you store the greens; if left on, it will inevitably bruise the leaves underneath.

The crispness of greens comes from the moisture in their leaf cells. As the greens get stale or warm, the cell walls weaken and the water starts to evaporate, taking with it the more subtle aspects of flavor and leaving the greens limp. But even then, all is not lost. If the cell walls have not been damaged by heat or freezing, some water can pass through them and fill the cells again. Greens that are only slightly limp can be revived by soaking them in cold water for a few minutes, then drying them and sticking them in the refrigerator for half an hour or so.

CLEANING GREENS Always be sure that whatever greens you use are thoroughly cleaned—nothing can ruin a salad faster than biting down on gritty greens. I like to clean batches of greens as soon as I pick them from the garden or bring them home from the market. The easiest way to do this is to place the greens in a large bowl or sink full of cold water and swish them around for thirty seconds or so. It's best to have enough water so the greens float several inches above the bottom. That way, as the grit is washed off, it will drift down to the bottom, well away from the greens.

After swishing, lift the greens from the water gently, drain the dirty water, and repeat the process until the water is clear. This may take only one rinsing for relatively clean greens like red leaf lettuce, or repeated rinsings for more grit-prone greens like spinach.

DRYING AND STORING GREENS Now we come to what may well be the most important thing about making a salad: dry the greens thoroughly after you wash them. If you dry greens properly, they will keep in the refrigerator for four or five days. Really. So you can go out to your garden, pick a big head of lettuce or a batch of other greens, clean and dry them, then be ready to make excellent salads the rest of the week. This method also works well if you don't have a garden but know some generous soul who does, because you have to visit the person only once in a while to have a continuing supply of greens.

Besides increasing storing capacity, there are two other very important reasons why greens should be well dried. First, any water left on the greens will dilute your dressing. Second, water will prevent the dressing from adhering to and coating the greens. As a result, you'll have a watery dressing that pools up separately from the greens, which is exactly what you don't want.

The best options for drying greens are either to roll them up in a cotton or linen towel, or whirl them in a salad spinner, fluff them up, and whirl them again. If you want to be a real stickler for dryness, use the salad spinner on the greens first, *then* roll them up in the towel and put them in the refrigerator for a few minutes. A final option is to use the method that my old roommate, George Cosette, claims he invented. Put the greens in a clean pillow case, then go stand outside and whirl it around your head. The George Method is incredibly effective... and it always impresses guests.

Once washed and dried, store your greens in whole leaves, then tear or cut them only when you are about to make a salad. Greens should be stored in the most humid part of the refrigerator, which is generally one of the vegetable storage bins. The ideal storage container is a muslin bag, which allows air to circulate freely around the greens. But since few of us have these bags, the second choice is to roll them loosely in paper towels right after you wash them, then put them into a plastic bag with holes poked in it.

But What If I Can't Find Arugula?

The one thing you really can't leave out of these recipes is some kind of green. And, in spite of the increasing availability of greens of all types in the United States, you may be unable to locate a particular green called for in a recipe. Don't worry about it. You can easily substitute another.

In fact, you can use just about any green in just about any recipe in this book, and you will still have a great salad. But there are some general rules of substitution that will keep the salad more or less in the flavor category that I had in mind.

Without worrying about subtleties, you can divide greens into three large categories: the "spicy" greens that have a peppery taste and/or a pleasant edge of bitterness; greens with more subtle flavors; and the cabbages.

The spicy or bitter greens include everything from arugula and endive to watercress and escarole to the wide range of Asian greens. Baby versions of "cooking greens" like turnip and kale also belong in this general grouping. These greens can be further subdivided into those that are quite peppery and those that are only mildly so.

Greens with more subtle flavors include, first and foremost, the large and varied family of lettuces. Basically, this family has four branches. The *butterhead lettuces*, like Boston and Bibb, are the most delicate, both in texture and flavor, with soft, thick leaves. *Looseleaf lettuces*—the most prolific variety, including red leaf, green leaf, oak leaf, and so on—are also somewhat delicate and are favored by gardeners because they produce a continuous succession of leaves rather than a head that goes to seed. *Cos lettuces*, like romaine, are cylindrical and upright, with a slightly coarser texture than butter-head or looseleaf. And last but most familiar, there is the sturdy, crisp, but almost tasteless iceberg, a primary example of the *crisp-head lettuces*.

Spinach also falls into the subtle flavor category, particularly when it is picked and eaten young.

In a third grouping, halfway between the subtle and the bitter greens, are the cabbages—red, green, savoy, and Chinese.

And basically, that's it. So here's the drill: when you can't find a green that is called for in a recipe, it is a safe bet to substitute any other green in the same category.

Of course, as with all rules there are some exceptions. Iceberg lettuce, with its crunchy, tasteless sturdiness, is in a category by itself. While it will work as a substitute for other lettuces, you'll probably have more success if you substitute leaf lettuces for each other and leave iceberg to itself. Then there are mixtures of baby greens, most often known by the French name of *mesclun*. You can substitute mixed mature greens of the tender variety, but you should try to get some of the bitter and some of the subtle into the mix, as well as contrasting textures.

Greens Groupings

The groupings below will allow you to substitute among greens and still stay very close to the flavors of the recipes as written, but don't feel bound by these categories; they are just general guidelines. In actual fact, it is fine to substitute fairly wildly among greens that are tender and mild enough to be eaten raw. As with all food, the most important factor is what tastes good to you.

Column B-1

The Mild Spicy Greens

Watercress (the
   mildest bunches)
Dandelion greens
   (ditto)
Arugula
Mizuna
Baby kale
Baby collards
Belgian endive

Column A

The Lettuces

Red leaf
Green leaf
Boston
Bibb
Oak leaf
Romaine
Any other
   variety you
   choose

Column B-2

*The Slightly
Spicier Greens*

Watercress (the most
   peppery bunches)
Dandelion greens
   (ditto)
Chicory
Escarole
Radicchio
Frisée
Curly endive
Tatsoi
Komatsu
Baby mustards
Baby turnip greens

For those who want more detail, here is a chart of substitutions. You'll notice that a couple of greens are in more than one category. And, as with most aspects of salads, you don't need to be too strict about this. If you're making a salad that calls for spinach and all you have is romaine or green leaf lettuce, just go ahead and use it. In almost all cases the salad will still be delicious.

Column D
The Cabbages
Green
Red
Savoy
Napa (Chinese)

Column C
Spinach
Spinach
Baby chard
Baby beet
greens

Column E
*Herbs as
Greens*
Parsley
Basil
Mint
Cilantro

Column F
No Substitutes
Iceberg lettuce
Purslane

The Dressings

Probably the most frequently asked question about salads is, "How much dressing should I use?" The answer to that, as with most culinary questions, is "As much as you want." As a rule of thumb, though, apply only enough dressing to lightly coat the greens and other ingredients. Like a good personal relationship, a proper salad should be a partnership, greens and dressing complementing each other with neither dominating. Fortunately for cooks, this equilibrium is easier to accomplish in the salad bowl than in the world of human relationships.

And just as you may misjudge people if you initially see them in the wrong context, so you may find some of the dressings here too intense if you taste them as if they were meant to be eaten by the spoonful. Remember that the dressings are much more powerful when tasted straight than they will be when they are transformed to a very thin coat on greens and other salad ingredients. To maintain enough of their power in that setting, they often need to start out very strong. So the best practice for tasting is to dip a piece of whatever green you will be using into the dressing. Even though that will still give you a more concentrated dose than you will experience in the actual salad, it's a closer approximation.

With very few exceptions, which are pointed out for you in the directions, the recipes in this book make more dressing than you will need for the particular salad the dressing accompanies. There are a couple of reasons for this. First, this allows those people who want to drown their salad in dressing to go ahead and do it. After all, it's your salad, and you can do what you want to it. More important, making extra dressing promotes conservation of effort—part of our constant attempt to "work smarter, not harder" in the kitchen. Mixing up dressings is not all that complicated or time-consuming, but it does take more time than the rest of the salad-building process. So why not mix up a large batch while you're at it?

In fact, many of the dressings in this book are actually like cold sauces, with all the flexibility and usefulness that term implies. Many are fantastic when tossed with individual vegetables, brushed on chicken on the grill, used as dips for vegetable sticks, drizzled over cold steak or hot pork chops, slathered onto a ham and cheese sandwich . . . the uses go on and on. Our recommendation is that you double each dressing recipe, so that you will have plenty left over for these other uses, as well as for dressing the salad.

Tossing the Salad

Once you've united dressing and salad, it's time to toss. The best tool for tossing salads is your hands. For those who want to avoid getting their hands oily, there is an excellent substitute, an indispensable aid to grilling: heavy-duty, spring-loaded tongs. As in grilling, the tongs act as a second pair of hands, with the added advantage that the cook can turn to another culinary task without having to stop and wash up. Whether with hands or tongs, the tossing action is the same. After applying the dressing, just grasp as much of the salad as you can and turn it top to bottom with a motion that resembles folding more than tossing. Continue turning for about thirty seconds before adding more dressing. Also, keep in mind that once a salad is tossed with its dressing, it really can't be kept long after the meal. So if you aren't sure all the salad is going to be eaten and you want to keep the leftovers, you can always toss the salad in the bowl without the dressing, then let people retoss on their individual plates. It's a little messy, but it's fun.

The Tools You Need

You will need the following tools to make almost every recipe in this book:

- ◆ Chef's knife
- ◆ Paring knife
- ◆ Chopping block
- ◆ Tongs
- ◆ Salad spinner and/or a cotton or linen towel

◆ A small bowl for mixing dressings

◆ A large bowl for tossing salads

As with all kitchen equipment, the better the tool the easier the work. So it's worth spending the money for a really good chef's knife and paring knife, and investing a little time and effort in sharpening them every once in a while. You'll be surprised at how much more quickly you can chop, slice, and dice. In the same vein, it is a lot more convenient to work on a large chopping block or cutting board, where you have plenty of room to chop up several onions or peppers or carrots. And as for the tongs, make sure you get the heavy-duty spring-loaded variety, rather than the type you have to physically open and close every time. When it comes to salad spinners, everyone has their favorite. Again, with salad spinners as with knives, spend a little extra money and get a sturdier version.

How Much Is in a "Head"? A "Bunch"?

There's a considerable difference in size among individual bunches or heads. The heads of cabbage or bunches of arugula at your local supermarket may be only half the size of the ones you find at the produce stand down the street, or vice versa.

Fortunately, salads are very forgiving, and it doesn't really matter that much if the head of lettuce you use is somewhat larger or smaller than the one I used. Decide for yourself how much lettuce should go in the salad, anyway, no matter what the recipe says.

But to give some guidelines about what these recipes mean when they call for "1 head" or "1 bunch," we kept track of the weight and volume of various greens as we used them. What we confirmed was the variability: bunches of watercress, for example, ranged from 4 to 7 ounces. We took the average weight for each type of green, then listed it in the following chart.

Average Weights of Commonly Used Greens

For the greens in this book that are bought by the head or the bunch rather than by the pound, this chart shows the average weight of the head or bunch as purchased, the weight after stems and any wilted or damaged leaves were trimmed, and the trimmed volume (loosely packed).

TYPE OF GREEN	WEIGHT UNTRIMMED	WEIGHT TRIMMED	VOLUME TRIMMED
Arugula	6 oz.	3.5 oz.	2.5 cups
Boston lettuce	5.25 oz.	4 oz.	2.5 cups
Cabbage, napa	2 lbs.	1 lb., 12 oz.	7 cups
Cabbage, red or green	2 lbs.	1 lb., 14 oz.	8 cups
Cabbage, savoy	1 lb., 14 oz.	1 lb., 10 oz.	7 cups
Dandelion greens	6.5 oz.	3.25 oz.	3 cups
Escarole	12.5 oz.	9 oz.	6 cups
Frisée	12 oz.	7.5 oz.	6 cups
Green leaf lettuce	11 oz.	7 oz.	4 cups
Radicchio	9.5 oz.	4.5 oz.	2 cups
Red leaf lettuce	10.25 oz.	7 oz.	4 cups
Romaine lettuce	14 oz.	9.25 oz.	4.5 cups
Spinach, curly leaf, packaged	10 oz.	8 oz.	7 cups
Spinach, flat-leaf, bunch	11 oz.	7.5 oz.	7 cups
Watercress	5 oz.	3 oz.	2.5 cups

Growing Your Own

It's fun to grow your own greens, not just because you get the satisfaction that always comes from raising your own food, but because you can plant all kinds of interesting greens that are almost impossible to find in stores. The more adventuresome seed companies can supply you with seeds for most of the Asian greens as well as for wilder greens like corn salad (mâche), orach, amaranth, quelite, miner's lettuce, and buckhorn plantain. Since you have control over when the greens are picked, you can also get the tiny baby versions of cooking greens like turnip greens, kale, collards, and broccoli rabe.

Besides, greens are very easy to grow. They are relatively pest resistant, can be planted early in the spring, and bear abundantly in spring, early summer, and autumn. Certain varieties last longer in the garden than just about anything other than root vegetables, and there are even some new varieties that do well in hot summer months. So growing greens gives us a big return on a small investment of time and energy. There are a number of excellent books that will help you learn to raise greens successfully—*The Salad Lover's Garden* by Sam Bittman and *Oriental Vegetables* by Joy Larkcom. For seeds, try any of these companies, all of which have high-quality seeds for interesting and unusual greens.

- ◆ The Cook's Garden, Box 65, Londonderry, VT 05148; 802-824-3400
- ◆ Johnny's Selected Seeds, Albion, ME 04910; 207-437-9294
- ◆ Nichols Garden Nursery, 1190 North Pacific Highway, Albany, OR 97321; 503-928-9280
- ◆ Seeds Blum, Idaho City Stage, Boise, ID 83707; 208-342-0858
- ◆ Shepherd's Garden Seeds, 6116 Highway 9, Felton, CA 95018; 408-335-6910; *or* 30 Irene Street, Torrington, CT 06790; 203-482-3638

There are a few additional points about these recipes that are probably worth mentioning, since they make a difference in how the salads come out.

First, most of the recipes in this book that use olive oil do not call for extra-virgin oil. The reason is simple: except in those instances where you really want the delicate, fruity flavor of the oil to come through, as in a simple vinaigrette, using extra-virgin is an ineffectual use of flavor. What you generally want the oil to pro-

Arugula Salad with Black Beans, Corn,
and Avocado with Orange-Chile Dressing

PAGE 108

Watercress and Radicchio Salad with Beets and
Leeks with Orange-Horseradish Dressing

PAGE 122

Arugula Salad with White Beans
and Shrimp with Basil Vinaigrette

PAGE 136

Watercress and Grilled Chicken Salad with Mangoes
and Grapes with Curry-Lime Vinaigrette

PAGE 159

Grandma Wetzler's Escarole Salad with Bacon,
Eggs, and Potatoes with Bacon-Vinegar Dressing

Green Leaf Lettuce with Grilled Peaches and Blue Cheese with Faux Catalina Dressing

Watercress Salad with Watermelon and Sweet-Sour Onion with A Very Simple Vinaigrette

Tomato and Bread Salad
with Lemon-Parsley Dressing

PAGE 252

Watercress Salad with Plums and Scallions with
Spicy Hoisin Dressing

PAGE 70

Arugula with Grilled Prosciutto
and Figs with Chunky
Roasted Pepper Vinaigrette

PAGE 242

Romaine Lettuce with Green Apples
and Stuffed Tortillas
with Citrus-Chipotle Dressing

PAGE 202

Parsley and Tomato Salad with Bulgur and Feta
Cheese with Simple Vinaigrette
PAGE 83

vide is a good, solid background flavor, so any good-quality pure olive oil is just fine. Plus, if you use extra-virgin oil only when you truly want its taste to shine, you can afford a really fine bottle.

Second, when a recipe calls for blanching ingredients like green beans or asparagus, you want to do this in such a way as to get the right texture without losing any of the flavor. Make sure the salted water is at a rolling boil before you toss in the ingredient. That way, it will get maximum heat with minimum soaking time. Also, when you put the water on to boil, at the same time fill a sink or big bowl with cold water with ice, so that as soon as you take the ingredient out of the boiling salted water, you can dunk it in the ice-cold water to stop the cooking process.

Third, a fair number of the salads in this book include one or more grilled ingredients. If the salad calls for grilled lamb chops, a few grilled chicken breasts, or several grilled fillets of fish, it is probably worth building a fire to cook just them. But if you are going to be grilling only a tomato or two or a single eggplant, it makes more sense to try to plan ahead and throw it on the grill when the fire is already lit to cook something else. Or, if it's the middle of the winter and you don't feel like lighting the grill, you can use the broiler as a substitute. If you decide to go the broiler route, you'll find that cooking times are approximately the same as for grilling, but just to be sure always check the broiled food for doneness, using the visual clues offered in the recipe instructions. And it's important that when you do grill, you do it over a fire of the right temperature for the food being cooked. That means you need to know how to check the fire temperature, which is very easy. After the fuel has gone through the red-hot stage and is covered with a fine film of gray ash, hold your hand about five inches above the grill surface: If you can hold it there for only one to two seconds, you have a hot fire; three to four seconds, a medium fire; and five to six seconds, a low fire.

So there you have it. You know everything you need; you've got the recipes right here. Go forth and make some great salads.

A GUIDE TO GREENS AND OTHER THINGS

The Greens Glossary

ARUGULA This spicy green, which originated in Italy, is also known as rocket, rucheta, or rucola. Its dark green leaves, which look somewhat like elongated oak leaves, have a distinctively rich, tangy, mildly peppery flavor that is an excellent foil for all kinds of other ingredients. The spiciness of arugula intensifies as it ages, and also varies considerably in intensity from bunch to bunch.

ASIAN GREENS There are literally hundreds of varieties of Asian greens. Virtually unknown outside ethnic Asian communities until the last decade or so, in the past few years they have begun to appear in mainstream markets. Their popularity was given a tremendous boost by their use in mesclun, the flavorful mixture of baby greens of all types that first became popular in California and now has spread across the country.

Asian greens actually have two advantages over lettuces of European ancestry. First, they do not turn brown when cut. This virtue results from the fact that, unlike lettuces, Asian greens contain very little lecithin, the substance in lettuces that seeps out when the leaves are cut and turns brown when it dries. Second, Asian greens dry more quickly than lettuces because they have smoother surfaces and therefore do not hold on to water.

With the exception of the green we know as Chinese cabbage, most Asian greens have a slightly bitter edge and need to be cooked when mature, but are delicious eaten raw when very young and tender. The following are some of the more popular Asian greens for use in salads.

Bok Choy, Baby Also known as pak choy or spoon cabbage, bok choy can be found in over twenty varieties in China. The three main types available in the United States are: white stemmed, which is the sturdiest of the three; soup spoon, named for its overlapping stems that resemble Chinese soup spoons and with a more delicate flavor than white stemmed; and green stemmed or Shanghai, which is the smallest, most fragile, and sweetest of the common varieties.

Chinese Cabbage Also known in the United States as celery cabbage because of its mild taste and crunchy texture, this cabbage is a staple ingredient in the diet of people in northern China, just as bok choy is for people in southern China. The two varieties most widely available in the United States are napa, with an oval, barrel-shaped head, and Michihli (named for a bay in northern China), with a long, cylindrical shape.

Chrysanthemum Leaves Perhaps the most unusual green to be found more and more frequently in American markets, chrysanthemum plants originated in the Mediterranean, but the leaves became popular as food only in Asia. The tangy-flavored, aromatic leaves, which come in flat or serrated versions, can be eaten raw when very small, but even then they are often blanched before use to make them less fibrous.

Komatsu Also known as mustard spinach, this green is actually a type of leafy turnip, with a flavor that is a cross between the blandness of cabbage and the bite of mustard.

Mizuna Among the best known of the Asian greens in the United States, mizuna has a mildly peppery flavor and dark green, feathery leaves that have given it the nickname of spider mustard. The seedlings are an essential addition to mesclun mixtures.

Mustard Greens, Baby Coarsest and most strongly flavored of the Asian greens, mustard greens come in literally hundreds of varieties. Tightly curled, rather stiff green mustard and flat-leafed purple varieties are among the most popular. Mustard greens can be eaten raw only when the leaves are very small, adding a rather intense peppery flavor to salad mixtures.

Pea Shoots These greens, which are simply the tendrils and top few leaves of regular pea stems, have a wonderful, delicate pea flavor. Very important in the cooking of Shanghai as well as the cuisine of Vietnam, they can be found in Asian markets throughout the United States.

Tatsoi or Rosette Bok Choy This ground-hugging member of the bok choy family derives its English name from the fact that its thick, very dark green leaves grow in tight, concentric circles like the petals of a rose. The individual leaves are oval, with a slightly more bitter flavor than standard bok choy, and in their baby form are widely used in mesclun mixtures.

CABBAGE (SEE ALSO CHINESE CABBAGE) Like most Americans, we use this term to refer to the headed cabbages with tightly furled leaves. The three primary varieties are red and green common cabbage, which have smooth leaves, and savoy cabbage, which has crinkly leaves. All have a crisp texture and mild but distinctive flavor.

CHICORY (CURLY ENDIVE) This term is somewhat confusing, because it refers not only to a family of greens (including frisée, radicchio, Belgian endive, dandelion greens, and escarole, among others) but also to a particular green, which in other parts of the country is called curly endive. Whatever you call it, this green has narrow, twisted, frilly leaves that are dark green at the top, fading to light green and eventually to white as you reach the stem. The leaves have a pronounced but pleasant bitterness. The outer leaves tend to be rather tough and should be cooked rather than eaten raw.

COOKING GREENS, BABY The term cooking greens refers to a whole group of greens that are usually cooked before being eaten (also known as pot herbs because the adult versions are thrown into the pot for cooking). They include the leafy tops of root vegetables like turnips and beets, as well as greens such as chard, kale, collard, and mustards. In their baby state, these greens are excellent in salads.

DANDELION GREENS Simply enough, these are the leaves of the dandelion, that yellow flower that is a pest in lawns but beautiful in the wild. The greens have a rich, pleasant flavor, bitter and rather sharp. One of the attractions of this green is that you can harvest it wild. Just make sure that you don't pick from an area where pesticides have been used or near roads, and pick only the tender young leaves, less than six inches long. Otherwise, buy dandelion greens at your produce market, where they are beginning to be more readily available.

ENDIVE (BELGIAN ENDIVE) Technically, the term endive refers to a whole family of greens. But most of us use it to mean Belgian endive, which is actually the blanched leaves of a type of chicory known as the witloof, grown in darkness to preserve its very light color and its mild flavor. The tightly furled heads of Belgian endive separate into narrow, cup-shaped leaves that have a bittersweet flavor typical of the chicory family, but milder than most others.

ESCAROLE Like other members of the chicory family, escarole has cut-edged leaves that are dark green at the top and grow paler as they approach the stem. The curving leaves of escarole, however, are broader than other chicories, resembling a butterhead lettuce. These inner leaves are excellent when eaten raw, with a nutty flavor that is less bitter than other chicories.

FRISÉE It's easy to remember the name of this member of the chicory family, because it actually looks frizzy. Its small, tender, delicately lacy pale green leaves with white centers have a milder bitterness and somewhat more delicate flavor than other members of the chicory clan.

LETTUCES There are hundreds of individual varieties of lettuce, with variation upon variation. Gardeners are familiar with dozens of favorites among the looseleaf varieties, such as Lolla Rossa, Black-seeded Simpson, Salad Bowl, Red Deer Tongue, and so on. But all lettuces fall within four general categories, classified by their shape and growth habit.

Butterhead Lettuces Including Boston and Bibb, these are known for their tender, softly folding, almost floppy leaves, which gather together into loose heads. These varieties have perhaps the most tender texture of all lettuces.

Crisphead For all intents and purposes, this term refers to the crisp, juicy, relatively flavorless iceberg lettuce, which for a couple of decades was what most Americans meant when they said "lettuce."

Cos Lettuces Romaine is the best known of this type, all of which are cylindrical and upright, with large ribs and a rather juicy but relatively coarse texture.

Looseleaf Lettuces A group that includes a wide variety, such as green leaf, red leaf, oak leaf, and so on, also known as bunching or cutting lettuces. These generic names derive from the fact that these lettuces do not grow as a head, but rather as a loose bunch of leaves. Instead of running to seed, they produce a continuous succession of leaves for cutting. That means gardeners can cut a handful of leaves every day, supplying their kitchens with salad greens through much of the summer.

MESCLUN This is not a type of green, but the name given to a mixture of salad greens that has recently become very popular in the United States. The term comes from the French word for "mixture," and the idea comes from the practice common through Europe (and much of the U.S. Southeast) of gathering a variety of young field greens and mixing them in a salad. Mesclun may include almost any green that is delicate and mild enough to be eaten raw, along with the occasional edible flowers or whole herb leaves. The trick is to get a nice balance between rather strong-flavored greens such as arugula or mizuna and blander greens such as baby lettuces, as well as a nice textural mix. Mesclun has been instrumental in introducing Americans to some wonderful Asian greens as well as to baby versions of arugula, mustard, chervil, and other spicy greens.

PURSLANE This green is a classic case of one person's weed being another's green. Widely eaten for centuries throughout India, Turkey, and parts of the Middle East, purslane has been considered a weed in the United States until very recently. Purslane looks like a small, creeping jade plant, with juicy stalks and small oval leaves that have a tart, lemony flavor.

RADICCHIO What we Americans call radicchio is actually a particular type of Italian chicory. This "green" has reddish-purple leaves bisected with white ribs and formed into a tight head that resembles a small, tender cabbage. Radicchio has a pleasant bitter flavor, and its unusual color also adds visual appeal to salads, which is one reason why it is a key ingredient in the salad mixture known as mesclun.

SPINACH Other than the lettuces, spinach is the green most familiar to Americans. Unfortunately, it had a bad reputation, largely because most of us ate it as a soggy, overcooked vegetable. Eaten raw, however, spinach is an excellent salad vegetable, with a distinctive taste that is very adaptable. Dark green spinach with very crinkly leaves is readily available in supermarkets in ten-ounce cellophane packages, and is quite acceptable. In spring and summer, though, you can find young, flat-leafed varieties, which have a fresher flavor, at produce stands and some markets.

WATERCRESS The most familiar of the large family of cresses, watercress has many small, dark green leaves on tender, rather leggy stems. Its peppery flavor varies in intensity from bunch to bunch.

General Glossary

BLACK BEANS Also known as turtle beans, these smooth-surfaced little legumes are a fixture of some South and Central American cuisines, particularly Mexican, Cuban, and Brazilian. The beans are available canned or dried in most U.S. supermarkets. The canned variety are perfectly acceptable, but are a bit mushy and don't have the full flavor of dried beans you cook yourself.

CHILE PEPPERS The varieties and types of chiles are many and bewildering: red, green, fresh, dried, superhot, sweet—you name it. Since there are more than 2,000 varieties of chile, each with its own heat level and individual flavor, it is useless to catalog them all here. In fact, you will notice that, when the recipes in this book call for fresh chiles, they specify a certain amount of "fresh chile pepper of your choice." Rather than search for a particular pepper for a given recipe, simply locate a variety you enjoy and that is readily available in your area, then develop a relationship with it. That way you will get to know just how hot a dish will be if you add a given amount of your favorite chile pepper. There are, however, a couple of chiles whose taste and heat are so distinctive that they should be used when specifically called for in a recipe, including the chipotle and the habanero. For more information on chile peppers, check one of the many excellent books that deal with the subject in detail: *The Whole Chile Pepper* (Little, Brown, 1990) by Dave Dewitt and Nancy Gerlach; *The Great Chile Book* by Mark Miller with John Harrison (Ten Speed Press, 1991); *Authentic Mexican* (Morrow, 1989) by Rick Bayless; and *Peppers: The Domesticated Capsicum* (University of Texas Press, 1984) by Jean Anderson.

CHIPOTLE PEPPERS Chipotles, which are dried, smoked jalapeño peppers, are flat and wrinkled, with a dark reddish-brown color, and 1 to 1½ inches long. Chipotles have a unique, imposing flavor that goes with everything and (particularly important for novice chile users) a consistent level of heat. They usually are found canned in *adobo* sauce, a mixture of onions, tomatoes, vinegar, and spices. You may however, find them dried. To use the dried variety, place them in very hot water and allow to soak for 40 minutes to reconstitute. In a real pinch, substitute a mixture of 1 pureed fresh chile pepper of your choice, 1 teaspoon catsup, and 1 drop Liquid Smoke for each chipotle called for.

CILANTRO Also known as fresh coriander, Mexican parsley, or Asian parsley, this pungent, very distinctive, highly aromatic herb is central to the cooking of Mexico, Latin America, and Southeast Asia. Since drying largely destroys the aromatic nature of cilantro, it is worth the effort to get the fresh herb.

CORIANDER SEEDS Like the leaves and stems (see Cilantro), the small, yellow-brown seeds of the coriander plant are widely used in Asian and Latin cooking. Lightly toasted and ground to a powder, the fruity, spicy, flowery seeds are an essential ingredient in curry powders as well as in many chutneys and sambals.

CUMIN SEEDS These greenish-yellow "seeds," with their distinctive, nutty flavor, are actually the ripe fruit of an annual herb of the same name. They are an integral part of the cooking of India, and are also widely used in Latin, African, and Middle Eastern cuisines. Their taste is similar to their cousin caraway, but is more musty. There is also a black variety of cumin, which has a sweeter, more refined, and more complex flavor, but it is expensive and difficult to locate.

DAIKON Although this root vegetable resembles a large, creamy white carrot, it is actually a radish. Crisp and juicy, with a sweet flavor and a very mild bite, it is extremely popular in Japan and China, and is usually eaten raw. Most daikon are between 6 and 15 inches long and from 2 to 3 inches in diameter, but some grow as large as footballs.

OLIVE OIL, EXTRA-VIRGIN After olives are harvested, they are pressed to release their oil. They are not run through this process just once, but several times. Extra-virgin olive oil is the oil that comes from the very first pressing of the olives. Since it also must, by definition, contain less than 1 percent acid, extra-virgin is the most mellow of olive oils. It is also the fruitiest and most flavorful. This is the one to use when the taste of the oil is really important, as in a simple vinaigrette.

FENNEL This plant comes in two varieties. Florence fennel, which has a large, bulbous base from which sprout long stalks with lacy fronds, is used as a vegetable. All parts of this plant of Mediterranean origins can be eaten, but the bulb is the part most often used. Delicious both raw and cooked, it has a mild licorice flavor with a slightly bitter aftertaste that is mellowed by roasting. Common fennel, which looks very much like Florence fennel without the bulb, is the source for fennel seeds, the greenish-brown, licorice-flavored oval seeds that are used as a spice.

FISH SAUCE Fish sauce is an essential ingredient in the cuisines of Southeast Asia. Known as *nuoc mam* in Vietnam, *nam pla* in Thailand, and *nam pa* in Laos, this thin, brownish sauce is made by packing anchovies or other small fish in salt and allowing them to ferment for three months or more, then drawing off the accumulated liquid. When used properly, it works much like salt in Western cooking, adding real depth of flavor without standing out as an individual taste.

FIVE-SPICE POWDER True to its name, this mixture—one of the most well known of the Asian spice blends—contains five spices: star anise, pepper, fennel seeds, cloves, and cinnamon. The mixture is very aromatic and quite powerful in flavor, though with relatively little heat.

HIZIKI A mild-flavored variety of seaweed (or sea vegetable, as these ocean-raised plants are now called), hiziki is very dark brown and wiry. Like arame, another sea vegetable which is almost identical to it, hiziki can be soaked in water before use, and should almost double in size while soaking.

HOISIN SAUCE One of the most popular sauces of Chinese cooking, this thick, sweetish, dark red mixture is composed of soybeans, garlic, vinegar, sugar, flour, chile, and various spices. Widely used as a table dipping sauce and in marinades, it can be found in all Chinese markets and many supermarkets.

JALAPEÑO PEPPER The jalapeño deserves special mention, as it is the best known and most widely consumed fresh chile in the United States. This pepper is plump and bullet-shaped, with a sleek, shiny exterior, 1 to 1½ inches long. Although relatively low on the heat scale of chiles, it still packs a decent punch. It is sold in both red and green stages of ripeness; although the red is a bit more difficult to locate, it has a richer flavor.

JICAMA The jicama is a bulbous root vegetable with a thin brown skin; a wonderful crisp, crunchy texture; and a sweetish taste that lies somewhere between an apple and a potato. It is widely used in the cooking of Mexico, Central and South America, and the Pacific coast of Asia. Peel its skin off with a knife, cover it with water, and jicama will keep, covered and refrigerated, for up to two days.

KOSHER SALT This coarse-grained salt, which contains natural iodine, is the type we recommend. We particularly like it in relishes because it dissolves more quickly than iodized salt, and because it has a better flavor than the free-flowing variety. Besides, it's more fun to sprinkle this stuff on with your fingers than to shake the standard variety out of a shaker.

LEMONGRASS This grass, grown throughout tropical Asia, provides a fresh, lemony, extremely aromatic flavor that is essential to the cuisines of Thailand and Vietnam. Lemongrass stalks have bulbs at the base like scallions, topped by long, thin, gray-green upper leaves. To prepare lemongrass, cut off the stems above the bottom third (the bulb) and reserve them for use in broths, soups, or teas. Remove the outer leaves from the bottom third of the stalk, and inside you will find a tender core. Mince this core very fine as you would ginger or garlic, and add to dishes as directed. Lemongrass can be found in Asian markets and is increasingly available in supermarkets.

MANGO This luscious, fragrant fruit comes in more varieties than apples—in India alone, 350 varieties are raised commercially—and is a daily staple in more than half of the world. Mangoes originated in the area around Burma, but today they are grown as a cash crop throughout the humid tropics, from India to Mexico to Central and South America and the Caribbean. Owing to the fruit's large pit and the slippery nature of its flesh, mango pulp can be somewhat difficult to get at, but it is well worth the effort.

PANCETTA This Italian bacon is cured with salt and spices but is not smoked. The kind most readily available is *pancetta arrotolata,* or "rolled pancetta," which comes in a roll that resembles a large sausage and is usually flavored with cloves and peppercorns.

PAPAYA The papaya, which looks somewhat like a melon in the shape of a pear, is native to the Caribbean (where it is also known as the pawpaw) and today is found in tropical regions throughout the world. The rind is pale green when unripe, becoming yellow when ripe; the musky-flavored, aromatic interior fruit ranges in color from greenish-yellow when under-ripe to bright orange or red when fully ripe. In the center of the fruit is a core of black seeds in a kind of slick gelatin; the seeds are edible, but are usually discarded. Like many tropical fruits, papaya is used as a vegetable when green and a fruit when ripe.

PLANTAIN This tropical relative of the banana is always cooked before being eaten, which is why it is sometimes called a cooking banana. In its green state, it has the starchy quality of a potato, but by the time it is ripe (the skin will blacken), the starch has turned to sugar. When ripe, plantains are used in desserts or as snack food; when green, they are most often cut into rounds and twice-fried. Plantains are most easily found in Latin and West Indian markets.

POMEGRANATE MOLASSES As the name implies, this is a thick syrup of concentrated pomegranate juice, with the deep, rich sweetness and sour undertones of the fruit from which it is made. It is available in Middle Eastern stores.

SESAME OIL Popular in Asian cooking, this oil is made from sesame seeds and has a pronounced, nutty, almost burned flavor. It is usually used for flavoring rather than straight cooking, often in combination with other, less flavorful oils.

STAR ANISE This star-shaped spice is the dried seed pod of an evergreen tree that grows in China and northern Vietnam. With its deep licorice flavor and its eight-pointed, star-shaped pod, it is one of the more exotic spices readily available to American cooks.

TAMARIND Tamarind trees, which reach heights of 70 feet, grow in the tropics throughout the world. Their fruit consists of pods from 3 to 6 inches long, covered with brown, furry skin and containing a dark pulp along with several seeds. The pulp has a tart, sweet-sour taste and is used in chutneys, curries, confections, stews, syrups, and drinks of all varieties. Tamarind is most easily located in paste form in Asian and Indian markets; it may also be found fresh or as syrup. When used in recipes, tamarind is usually diluted to make tamarind water. If you absolutely can't locate tamarind, you can substitute equal parts fresh lime juice, molasses, and Worcestershire sauce.

VINEGARS Vinegars are created by a double fermentation process. During the first part of the process, the sugars in liquids such as apple juice and grape juice are turned to alcohol. In the second part, yeast cells are introduced into the liquid and turn the alcohol to acetic acid. Vinegars are excellent flavor balancers, adding a sour taste that brings other flavors into harmony. There are many kinds of vinegar, of which the following are used in this book:

Apple Cider Vinegar This vinegar, quite popular for its earthy flavor, is made from fermented apple juice.

Balsamic Vinegar Mellow and complex, balsamic vinegar is a distinctly flavored red wine vinegar. True balsamic is aged in wooden casks, and the contents of several different casks are combined during the aging process to create the final product. This time-consuming process makes true balsamic not only more complex and tasty but also more expensive than the ersatz version found in most supermarkets. The best way to decide if the brand is worth the money is to buy one bottle and check it out.

Red Wine Vinegar The name says it—it's made from red wine. Brands vary wildly in quality, depending on the wine used and the aging process. The most expensive red wine vinegars are aged in wooden vats.

Rice Wine Vinegar The Asian version of red wine vinegar, this is made from fermented rice water and has a beautifully delicate, subtle taste.

Sherry Vinegar This is simply vinegar made from sherry. As you might expect, it has a somewhat richer, nuttier, more complex flavor than vinegars made from nonfortified wines.

White, or Distilled, Vinegar Like vodka, this garden-variety vinegar is made from grains. It is the least subtle of vinegars, made through a quick distillation process.

WASABI Basically a Japanese form of horseradish, this pale green condiment is available as either a powder or a paste. It has a sharper bite and more pungent flavor than the white horseradish of the West. Wasabi is smeared over the rice in sushi before the fish is added, and is usually served alongside sashimi.

The Pantry of Four: Basics to Have on Hand

HOMEMADE MAYONNAISE You can always use prepared may-onnaise, but the flavor of the homemade version is so much fresher that it's worth whipping up a batch every once in while. There's not all that much to it, particularly if you have a food processor or blender. Just combine two egg yolks, one tablespoon of fresh lemon juice, salt and pepper to taste, and a couple tablespoons of extra-virgin olive oil in the bowl of your processor or blender and turn on the machine. Then add a little less than a cup of extra-virgin olive oil in a slow, steady stream. Like magic, it will form a thick, creamy emulsion. If the mixture ends up being a little too thick, add about a tablespoon or two of warm water to thin it. Of course, you can also make mayon-naise using a whisk and bowl if you are a purist. In either case it will keep, covered and refrigerated, for up to a week.

Although relatively minor, there is some danger of salmonella when eating uncooked egg yolks. Pregnant women, the elderly, infants, and people whose immune systems are compromised should avoid raw eggs. For others, it is simply a matter of bal-ancing the risk versus the pleasure. If you want mayonnaise with-out risk, cook two egg yolks, one teaspoon lemon juice, one teaspoon water, and salt and pepper to taste in a saucepan over very low heat, stirring constantly, until the mixture bubbles in one or two places. Let stand four minutes, pour into the blender or food processor, and proceed to add the oil as described.

OVEN-DRIED TOMATOES Drying tomatoes concentrates their flavor and makes them even sweeter. To dry plum tomatoes, split them in half lengthwise, rub them lightly with olive oil, and sprinkle them with salt and pepper. Place the tomatoes skin side down in a single layer on a drying rack set on top of a sheet pan, then place the pan on the middle rack of a 200°F. oven for six to eight hours. The tomatoes should be reduced in size by about one-quarter, shriveled up on the outside but still tender and juicy on the inside. They may be stored, covered and refrigerated, for four to five days.

ROASTED GARLIC Rub the whole head of garlic a bit in your hands to remove some of the papery outer peel. Slice the top ¼ inch off the garlic, exposing the tips of the individual cloves, and place the whole head in the middle of a foot-long sheet of aluminum foil. Pour two tablespoons olive oil over the top of the garlic, then wrap it up tightly. Place in a 300°F. oven and roast for about one hour, or until the individual garlic cloves are soft to the touch. To extract the garlic meat from the roasted head, just squeeze the cloves at the base and the rich, mellow meat will shoot right out.

ROASTED RED BELL PEPPERS Place the peppers on the grill over a hot fire or on top of a gas stove burner turned to high. Roll them around until the skin is completely dark and well blistered. Remove from the flame, place in a brown paper bag, tie the bag shut, and allow the peppers to cool in the bag for about thirty minutes to loosen the skin. Remove the peppers from the bag and slide the skin off with your fingers. Tear the peppers in half, remove the inner cores and seeds, and run the peppers gently under cold water to remove any remaining charred pieces of skin. Put into a small container, add olive oil to cover, cover the container, and refrigerate. Peppers will keep several weeks when stored in this manner.

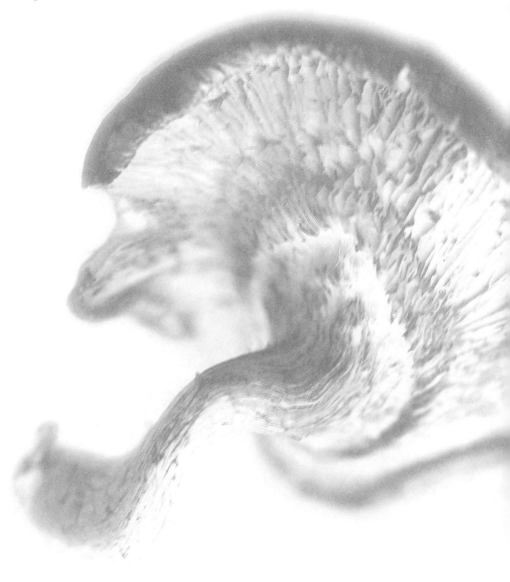

3
SIMPLE SALADS

THE RECIPES IN THIS CHAPTER might be thought of as the essence of salads. Every one is easy, quick, and healthful. Each contains only a few ingredients, but they all have a lot of bold, interesting flavors. In fact, these salads make the case that simple does not have to mean boring.

Some of them, like the Iowa Lettuce Salad or Grandma Wetzler's Escarole Salad with Bacon, Eggs, and Potatoes, are legacies from the days when our grandparents depended on local ingredients and seldom used oil. Others, like Cary's Leaf Lettuce Salad with Orange, Fennel, and Red Onion or Watercress Salad with Plums and Scallions, are simple combinations of ingredients inspired by the flavor palates of Mediterranean, Asian, or Latin American cuisines. Others, like Regulation Caesar Salad with Lots of Garlic Croutons or Your Classic Wedge of Iceberg, are tasty versions of the classic salads that we all grew up with.

Whichever of these salads you choose, you won't have to spend much time in the kitchen getting a salad on the table. And remember that, although some of the dressings involve a little chopping and mixing, or may require you to do something like cook a few pieces of bacon, if you make extra dressing you will find plenty of other uses for it, so the time-to-result ratio is still right up there.

Iowa Lettuce Salad

WITH SIMPLE CREAM DRESSING

Summer Sunday dinner at my Grandma Schwyhart's Iowa farm was always the same—crispy fried chicken, mashed potatoes with chicken gravy, thick slices of sun-warmed tomatoes, and for dessert home-churned vanilla ice cream. With this, there was always the same green salad—leaf lettuces straight from the garden, lightly coated with a mixture of vinegar, sugar, and cream, a legacy from the days when oil was too rare to be used on salads. This dressing will also make a sweet but classy cole slaw.

S E R V E S 4 T O 6

Best substitute greens: Any from Column A, page 18.

For the dressing

¼ cup white vinegar

¼ cup sugar

2 tablespoons light cream

2 teaspoons celery seeds

Salt and freshly cracked black pepper to taste

For the salad

1 small head Bibb or butter lettuce, washed, dried, and leaves torn in half

1 small head oak leaf or red leaf lettuce, washed, dried, and leaves torn in half

1. In a small bowl, combine all the dressing ingredients and mix vigorously with a fork until the sugar is dissolved.

2. In a large bowl, combine the lettuces. Stir the dressing well, add just enough to moisten the lettuce, toss to coat, and serve.

Your Classic Wedge of Iceberg

WITH THOUSAND ISLAND DRESSING

These days, iceberg lettuce has a lousy reputation, justly deserved after decades of appearing in third-rate salads in restaurants and homes across America. But don't overlook the virtues of this sturdy, easily transportable lettuce. Just as the best hot dog can be an outstanding eating experience, a wedge of fresh, crisp, juicy iceberg lettuce topped with a homemade version of thousand island dressing is nothing for food snobs to dismiss out of hand. Try spreading this dressing on your grilled cheese sandwich.

S E R V E S   4   T O   6

For the dressing

1   cup mayonnaise, yours or mine (page 41)

2   tablespoons apple cider vinegar

¼   cup catsup

2   tablespoons pickle relish

1   stalk celery, diced fine

2   hard-cooked eggs, diced fine

¼   cup roughly chopped fresh parsley

4   dashes Tabasco sauce

2   dashes Worcestershire sauce

Salt and freshly cracked black pepper to taste

For the salad

1   head iceberg lettuce, cut into 4 to 6 wedges, depending on the size of the head

In a medium bowl, combine all the dressing ingredients and mix well. Drizzle generously over each wedge of iceberg and serve with a knife and fork.

Salad of Young Cooking Greens
WITH WARM PANCETTA DRESSING

The division between salad greens and cooking greens is mainly one of toughness. When mature, greens like kale, collard, turnip, and mustard are too tough and bitter to eat raw. In their baby state, though, these so-called cooking greens (also known as pot herbs) are excellent in salads. This is a wonderful way to use tiny leaves of chard and baby beet and turnip greens. This dressing also works well on warm potato salad.

S E R V E S   4   T O   6

Best substitute greens: Any edible young greens.

For the dressing

6	slices pancetta or meaty bacon
½	cup olive oil
¼	cup apple cider vinegar
1	tablespoon sugar
	Salt and freshly cracked black pepper to taste

For the salad

About 1 pound very young cooking greens (turnip, mustard, kale, collard, beet, or chard), trimmed, washed, and dried

1. In a medium sauté pan, cook the pancetta or bacon over medium-high heat until crisp, 6 to 8 minutes. Remove the pan from the heat and drain off the fat, but leave the bacon or pancetta in the pan. Add the oil, vinegar, sugar, and salt and pepper, return to heat, and bring just to a boil. Remove from the heat.

2. Place the young greens in a large bowl. Pour the hot dressing over the greens, toss well, and serve at once.

Local Salad Johnson

WITH SHALLOT VINAIGRETTE

Our good buddy Steve Johnson, a super-talented Boston chef, spends many hours prowling the fields of local farmers in search of their best produce for his restaurant. Steve created this particular salad for a cookout held to bene-fit Coastal Growers, a farmer's cooperative in Westport, Massachusetts. It has all the qualities needed to join the long line of "Johnson" dishes: quick, easy, and with outstanding flavor. This dressing also makes an excellent pasta salad.

S E R V E S   4   T O   6

Best substitute greens: In the spirit of the dish, use whatever lettuces or greens are available from local farmers in your area.

For the dressing

- ¼ cup sherry vinegar
- 1 teaspoon Dijon mustard
- 1 teaspoon kosher salt
- ½ teaspoon freshly cracked black pepper
- 2 shallots, peeled and thinly sliced
- Kernels of corn from 1 ear
- ¼ cup thinly sliced fresh basil
- ⅔ cup olive oil

For the salad

- 1 small head oak leaf or Boston lettuce, trimmed, washed, dried, and leaves torn in half
- 1 bunch arugula, trimmed, washed, and dried
- 1 small (pickling) cucumber, peeled
- 3 scallions, trimmed and sliced on the bias (white and green parts)
- 2 ripe medium tomatoes, cored and cut into eighths

1. In a small bowl, whisk together the vinegar and mustard. Add the salt, pepper, and shallots. Allow to stand for about 5 minutes so the shallots soften a bit. Add the corn, basil, and olive oil and whisk together. Allow to stand, covered, for about 30 minutes before using so that the corn kernels soften slightly.

2. In a large bowl, combine the lettuce, arugula, cucumber, scallions, and tomatoes. Stir the dressing well, add just enough to moisten the ingredients (there will be some dressing left over), toss to coat, and serve.

Salad of Boston Lettuce, Mango, Cucumber, and Avocado

WITH CREAMY ORANGE-SPICE DRESSING

In the tropics, salads combining fruits with vegetables are very popular. This salad, for example, was inspired by rojak, *a popular Malaysian dish in which a spicy sauce is mixed with fruits, usually including mangoes, and vegetables, almost always including cucumbers. The dressing used here is also good spooned over avocados, as a cole slaw dressing, or a slightly wild sandwich spread.*

S E R V E S   4

Best substitute greens: Any from Column A, page 18.

For the dressing

- ½   cup mayonnaise, yours or mine (page 41)
- ½   cup fresh orange juice (about 1 large orange)
- 2   tablespoons fresh lime juice (about 1 medium lime)
- 2   tablespoons cumin seeds, toasted in a sauté pan over medium heat, shaking, until fragrant, 2 to 3 minutes (or substitute 1 tablespoon ground cumin)
- 1   tablespoon coriander seeds, toasted in a sauté pan over medium heat, shaking, until fragrant, 2 to 3 minutes (or substitute ½ tablespoon ground coriander)
- 8   dashes Tabasco Sauce
- ¼   cup roughly chopped fresh cilantro
     Salt and freshly cracked black pepper to taste

For the salad

- 1   head Boston lettuce, any tough outer leaves discarded, inner leaves washed, dried, and torn in half
- 1   mango, peeled, pitted, and diced large
- 1   avocado, peeled, pitted, and diced large
- 1   cucumber, peeled if you want to, diced large

1. In a medium bowl, combine the mayonnaise, orange juice, and lime juice and whisk until well blended. Add the remaining dressing ingredients and mix well.

2. In a large bowl, combine the lettuce, mango, avocado, and cucumber. Stir the dressing well, add just enough to moisten the ingredients (there will be some dressing left over), toss to coat, and serve.

Grandma Wetzler's Escarole Salad with Bacon, Eggs, and Potatoes

WITH BACON-VINEGAR DRESSING

Escarole is like a broader, flatter version of curly endive. The outer leaves tend to be quite tough, so it's best to remove and save them for some other use in which they are cooked. My Grandma Wetzler, who has put more good food on the table than any professional chef I know, used to make this dressing (with apple cider vinegar) in the days before oil was common enough to be used in salad dressings.

S E R V E S   4   T O   6

Best substitute greens: Any from Column B-2, page 18.

For the dressing

- 4 slices bacon
- ⅓ cup sugar
- ½ cup balsamic vinegar
- ¼ cup olive oil

For the salad

- 1 large bunch escarole, tough outer leaves removed, inner leaves trimmed, washed, and dried
- 12 small Red Bliss potatoes (about the size of golf balls), cooked in boiling water until easily pierced with a fork, about 15 minutes, then halved
- 2 hard-cooked eggs, roughly chopped

1. In a sauté pan over medium-high heat, cook the bacon until crisp, 6 to 8 minutes. Remove from the heat, drain on paper towels, crumble, and set aside. Discard about half the bacon drippings from the pan, add the sugar, vinegar, and oil to the remaining drippings, and bring to a boil over high heat. Remove the pan from the heat.

2. Place the escarole in a large bowl. Pour the warm dressing over the top, add the potatoes, and toss to coat.

3. Transfer the dressed escarole and potatoes to a serving platter or individual plates, sprinkle with the bacon and egg, and serve at once.

Cary's Leaf Lettuce Salad with Orange, Fennel, and Red Onion

WITH GREEN OLIVE DRESSING

With its crunchy texture and subtle licorice flavor, raw fennel is a great salad ingredient. The key is to slice it very, very thin. My business partner Cary Wheaton, who always puts on an incredible spread at her house, recently served this salad at the beginning of a celebratory meal; unfortunately, people liked it so much, and ate so much of it, that they couldn't do justice to the lobster chowder and grilled tenderloin that followed. The Moroccan-inspired dressing is also excellent as a dressing for a pasta salad or white bean salad.

S E R V E S   4   T O   6

Best substitute greens: Any from Column A, page 18.

For the dressing

- ¾ cup extra-virgin olive oil
- ¼ cup red wine vinegar
- ⅓ cup pitted and roughly chopped green olives (picholine, sevillano, cracked Moroccan, etc.)
- 1 teaspoon minced garlic
- 2 tablespoons coriander seeds, toasted in a sauté pan, shaking, until fragrant, 2 to 3 minutes (or substitute 1 tablespoon ground coriander)
- 1 teaspoon ground cinnamon
- ¼ cup finely chopped fresh parsley
  Salt and freshly cracked black pepper to taste

For the salad

- 1 large head leaf lettuce (Bibb, Boston, red leaf, etc.), washed, dried, and leaves torn in half
- 2 oranges, seeded, peeled, and cut into ½-inch slices
- 1 medium red onion, peeled, halved, and halves very thinly sliced

1 large bulb fennel, fronds and root end trimmed off,
   rest of bulb very thinly sliced lengthwise
   Salt and freshly cracked black pepper to taste

1. In a small bowl, combine all the dressing ingredients and whisk together well.

2. In a large bowl, combine the lettuce, oranges, onion, fennel, and salt and pepper. Stir the dressing well, add just enough to moisten the ingredients (there will be some dressing left over), toss well, and serve.

Regulation Caesar Salad with Lots of Garlic Croutons

Reputed to have been invented in northern Mexico by a chef named Caesar, this romaine-based salad has gone on to become the single most popular salad in America. This makes sense, since the salad has some real flavor as well as a story that goes with it, and is simple to prepare. The technique of cooking the eggs just slightly so they remain quite runny is derived from the infamous Turkish "doggy eggs" of our buddy Ihsan Gurdal. This dressing also makes an outstanding pairing with grilled or poached chicken or vegetable sticks.

SERVES 4 TO 6

For the dressing

- 2 large eggs
- ½ cup extra-virgin olive oil
- 1 teaspoon minced garlic
- ¼ cup fresh lemon juice (about 1 large lemon)
- 4 anchovies, minced (optional)
- 3 dashes Worcestershire sauce
- Salt and freshly cracked black pepper to taste

For the salad

- 2 cups bread cubes, in about ½-inch squares
- ⅓ cup olive oil
- 1 tablespoon minced garlic
- 2 tablespoons roughly chopped fresh parsley
- Salt and freshly cracked black pepper to taste
- 1 medium head romaine lettuce, tough outer leaves removed, inner leaves washed, dried, and torn in halves or thirds
- ⅓ cup grated Parmesan cheese

1. Slip the eggs into a small saucepan of boiling water and boil for just 2 minutes. Remove the eggs from the water and crack the yolks into a small bowl. Add all remaining dressing ingredients and whisk to combine. Set aside.

2. Put the bread cubes into a large bowl. In a small bowl, combine the oil, garlic, parsley, and salt and pepper and mix well. Pour this mixture over the bread cubes and toss well to coat the cubes. Place on an ungreased baking sheet and bake in a 350°F. oven until crunchy on the outside but still chewy on the inside, 10 to 12 minutes.

3. Place the romaine in a large bowl. Stir the dressing well, add just enough to moisten the lettuce (there will be some dressing left over), and toss to coat. Add the seasoned croutons, sprinkle with cheese, and serve.

Southwestern Caesar Salad

WITH CREAMY CHILE DRESSING

This spicy Southwestern take on the ever-popular Caesar salad is a more substantial preparation, enough for a summer meal all by itself. If you want to torque it up even more, toss in some slices of cold grilled or roasted chicken. I think cornbread makes the best croutons, but you can use any type you like. This dressing is also great used over baked sweet potato.

S E R V E S   4   T O   6

For the dressing

- ¼   cup sour cream
- ½   cup olive oil
- ¼   cup fresh lime juice (about 2 medium limes)
- ¼   cup roughly chopped fresh cilantro
- 2   tablespoons chili powder
- 1   teaspoon minced garlic
- 1   tablespoon minced fresh chile pepper of your choice

    Salt and freshly cracked black pepper to taste

For the salad

- ⅓   cup olive oil
- 1   teaspoon minced garlic
- 2   tablespoons cumin seeds
    (or substitute 1 tablespoon ground cumin)
- 2   cups diced cornbread, in ½-inch cubes,
    or other bread of your choice
- 1   head romaine lettuce, outer leaves removed, inner leaves washed, dried, and torn in halves or thirds
- 2   avocados, peeled, pitted, and quartered
- 2   medium tomatoes, cored and quartered
- 1   small red onion, peeled, halved, and thinly sliced
- ⅓   cup grated Parmesan cheese

1. In a small bowl, combine the sour cream and olive oil, and whisk together (it will look a little curdled, but don't worry). Add the remaining dressing ingredients and whisk to blend (now it should be smooth). Set aside.

2. In a large bowl, combine the olive oil, garlic, and cumin and mix well. Add the bread cubes and toss well to coat. Put the seasoned cubes on an ungreased baking sheet and bake in a 350°F. oven until crisp on the outside but still chewy inside, about 10 minutes.

3. In a large bowl, combine the romaine lettuce, avocados, tomatoes, and onion. Stir the dressing well, add just enough to moisten the ingredients (there will be some dressing left over), and toss to coat. Sprinkle with cheese and croutons, and serve.

Arugula, Grapefruit, and Orange Salad
WITH SIMPLE LEMON VINAIGRETTE

This simple salad of greens and citrus is so good that we have been trading it back and forth with our friend Mark Bittman for years. If you have the time and inclination, peel the membrane off the grapefruit and orange sections. If you prefer your salads a little sweeter, try substituting one drained can of mandarin oranges for the orange. Since Mark is also the author of the excellent book Fish *(Macmillan, 1994), try drizzling this dressing on a piece of grilled tuna or swordfish.*

S E R V E S   4   T O   6

Best substitute greens: Any from Column B-1, page 18.

For the dressing

- ½ cup olive oil
- ¼ cup fresh lemon juice (about 1 large lemon)
- ¼ cup roughly chopped fresh parsley
- 1 teaspoon minced garlic
- Salt and freshly cracked black pepper to taste

For the salad

- 1 grapefruit, peeled, separated into sections, and sections halved
- 1 orange, peeled, separated into sections, and sections halved
- 1 red onion, halved and very thinly sliced
- 1 bunch arugula, trimmed, washed, and dried
- ¼ cup loosely packed whole fresh basil leaves
- 2 tablespoons toasted sesame seeds (optional)
- Pomegranate seeds for garnish (optional)

1. In a small bowl, combine all the dressing ingredients and whisk together well.

2. In a large bowl, combine the grapefruit, orange, onion, arugula, and basil leaves. Stir the dressing well, add just enough to moisten the ingredients (there will be some dressing left over), and toss to coat. Sprinkle with sesame seeds and pomegranate seeds if you have them, and serve.

Arugula Salad with Dried Tomatoes, Grilled Red Onions, and Parmesan

WITH CREAMY BALSAMIC DRESSING

If you have oven-dried tomatoes in your refrigerator—which is always a good idea—this salad will take about five minutes to put together. It's a classic for a hot summer evening dinner, along with some crusty bread and a nice grilled steak. As a matter of fact, this dressing is also excellent served on steak, warm or cold.

S E R V E S 4

Best substitute greens: Any from Column B-1, page 18.

For the dressing

- ¼ cup pitted Kalamata or other briny black olives, roughly chopped
- ¼ cup grainy mustard
- 1 teaspoon minced garlic
- ¾ cup olive oil
- ¼ cup balsamic vinegar
- ¼ cup roughly chopped fresh basil
  Salt and freshly cracked black pepper to taste

For the salad

- 2 red onions about the size of baseballs, peeled and cut into ½-inch rings
- 2 tablespoons olive oil
  Salt and freshly cracked black pepper to taste
- 2 bunches arugula, trimmed, washed, and dried
- 12 oven-dried plum tomatoes (page 41; or substitute 6 fresh plum tomatoes), halved
- ¼ cup grated Parmesan cheese

1. Prepare a medium-hot fire in your grill.

2. Put the olives, mustard, and garlic in a food processor or blender and puree. With the motor still running, add the olive oil in a steady stream, then turn off the motor. Add the balsamic vinegar and basil, pulse to combine, season with salt and pepper, and set aside.

3. Coat the onions lightly with oil and sprinkle with salt and pepper. Grill the onions over medium-high heat until well browned, 3 to 4 minutes per side. Remove from the heat.

4. In a large bowl, combine the arugula, dried tomatoes, and grilled onions. Stir the dressing well, add just enough to moisten the ingredients (there will be some dressing left over), and toss to coat. Place on a platter or individual serving plates, sprinkle with Parmesan, and serve.

Roasted Pear and Chicory Salad
WITH CHUNKY BLUE CHEESE DRESSING

Just two ingredients in this salad plus a dressing, and you still get different tastes in every bite. Roasting the pears deepens their intrinsic flavor and adds a caramel taste; and, like all the bitter greens, chicory (also known as curly endive) has a whole complex of flavors going for it. The blue cheese dressing is excellent spread on roast beef or ham sandwiches.

SERVES 4 TO 6

Best substitute greens: Any from Column B-2, page 18.

For the dressing

- ¾ cup olive oil
- ¼ cup apple cider vinegar
- ⅓ cup roughly crumbled blue cheese of your choice
- ¼ cup finely chopped fresh oregano
  (or substitute parsley)
- 4 dashes Tabasco sauce
- 6 dashes Worcestershire sauce
  Salt and freshly cracked black pepper to taste

For the salad

- 2 pears of your choice, halved and cored
- 2 tablespoons vegetable oil
  Salt and freshly cracked black pepper to taste
- 1 head chicory, washed, dried, and leaves torn in half

1. Preheat the oven to 350°F.

2. In a medium bowl, combine all dressing ingredients and whisk together well. Set aside.

3. Rub the pears with the vegetable oil and sprinkle them with salt and pepper. Place the pears on a lightly greased baking sheet and roast in the oven until lightly browned, 30 to 35 minutes. Remove from the oven and, as soon as they are cool enough to handle, slice each pear half into 3 or 4 slices.

4. In a large bowl, combine the pear slices with the chicory and season with salt and pepper. Stir the dressing well, add just enough to moisten the chicory and pears (there will be some dressing left over), toss to coat, and serve.

Dandelion Greens with Nectarines and Smithfield Ham

WITH PEANUT-MOLASSES DRESSING

If you live in an area where dandelions grow free of pesticides, you can gather your own dandelion leaves in the early spring. Just be sure that you pick the small leaves; dandelion leaves more than about six inches long are too bitter to eat raw. Whether you gather them or buy them, be sure to rinse them very well, as they are often quite sandy. In this salad, the sweet dressing helps balance the sharpness of the dandelion greens. Believe it or not, I would use this dressing on cole slaw, roast pork, or a ham sandwich. Try it.

S E R V E S   4   T O   6

Best substitute greens: Any from Column B-1, page 18.

For the dressing

¾	cup olive oil
¼	cup apple cider vinegar
¼	cup molasses
¼	cup finely chopped unsalted toasted peanuts
2	tablespoons finely chopped fresh sage
	Salt and freshly cracked black pepper to taste

For the salad

	About 1 pound young, tender dandelion greens, trimmed, washed, and dried
2	nectarines, pitted and each cut into 8 slices
1	small red onion, peeled, halved, and thinly sliced
8	ounces Smithfield ham, thinly sliced (or substitute any other country ham or prosciutto)

1. In a small bowl, combine all the dressing ingredients and whisk together until well blended.

2. In a large bowl, combine the dandelion greens, nectarines, onion, and ham. Stir the dressing well, pour on just enough to moisten the ingredients (there will be some dressing left over), toss to coat, and serve.

Watercress Salad with Plums and Scallions

WITH SPICY HOISIN DRESSING

The combination of ingredients in this Asian-inspired salad has it all—spicy, hot, sweet, slightly bitter . . . you name it, and it's here. At the same time, the salad is simple to put together and healthful, to boot. If you want an even simpler salad, watercress alone, lightly coated with this dressing, is also excellent. The dressing is also good to use as a dip with raw vegetables or serve alongside roast chicken.

SERVES 4 TO 6

Best substitute greens: Any from Column B-2, page 18.

For the dressing

¼ cup hoisin sauce

½ cup olive oil

¼ cup rice wine vinegar (or substitute white wine vinegar)

1 tablespoon minced fresh ginger

1 tablespoon minced orange zest (no white)

1 tablespoon minced fresh chile pepper
of your choice

1 tablespoon freshly cracked white pepper
(or substitute black pepper)
Salt to taste

For the salad

2 bunches watercress, trimmed, washed, and dried

3 ripe but firm plums, pitted and quartered

5 scallions, roots trimmed, thinly sliced lengthwise
(green and white parts)

1 red bell pepper, halved, seeded, and
thinly sliced lengthwise

2 tablespoons sesame seeds, toasted in a 350°F. oven,
shaken frequently, until browned, about 10 minutes

1. Put the hoisin sauce in a small bowl. Add the olive oil in a steady stream while whisking steadily. Add all the remaining dressing ingredients and whisk to combine.

2. Place all the salad ingredients except sesame seeds in a large bowl. Pour on enough of the dressing to just moisten the ingredients (there will be some dressing left over) and toss to coat. Place the dressed salad on a platter or individual serving plates, sprinkle with the sesame seeds, and serve.

Watercress Salad with Watermelon and Sweet-Sour Onion

WITH A VERY SIMPLE VINAIGRETTE

The idea of using watermelon in a savory way was something I learned at an early age, as I watched my grandfather eat his watermelon with salt and pepper. So it really bummed me out one day when I walked into the restaurant of my friend Gordon Hamersley and saw on the menu a savory watermelon salad. Why hadn't I thought of that? Since that time I have used Gordon's idea so often that I have a hard time remembering that it wasn't my own idea to begin with. It's truly delicious, but if for some reason you don't like it, that's when I'll remember that it was Gordon's concept; you should give him a call at his outstanding eatery in Boston's South End.

S E R V E S   4   T O   6

Best substitute greens: Any from Column B-1, page 18.

For the dressing

¾   cup extra-virgin olive oil

¼   cup red wine vinegar

     Salt and freshly cracked black pepper to taste

For the salad

1   medium red onion, peeled and thinly sliced

⅓   cup fresh lime juice (about 3 medium limes)

⅓   cup red wine vinegar

2   tablespoons sugar

1   bunch watercress, trimmed, washed, and dried

1   loosely packed cup fresh flat-leaf parsley, washed and dried

1   cup diced watermelon, in ½-inch cubes, seeds removed

1. In a small bowl, whisk together the olive oil and vinegar, and season with salt and pepper. Set aside.

2. In a small bowl, combine the onion, lime juice, vinegar, and sugar and set aside for 2 hours.

3. In a large bowl, combine the watercress, parsley, and watermelon. Add just enough dressing to moisten the ingredients (there will be some dressing left over) and toss to coat. Place the salad on a large platter or individual serving plates. Drain the onion, place on top of the salad, and serve.

Lettuce of Choice with Grilled New Potatoes and Red Onion Rings

WITH SPICY BALSAMIC VINAIGRETTE

From East Coast Grill chef Ken Goodman, who understands that simple is often best, comes this salad, which tastes great not only with any lettuce you want to use but with just about any green at all. If you're ever in the Grill, stop back and say hi to Ken—he's the guy with the grin and the dreadlocks, who's standing over the fire. Drizzle this aromatic dressing over roasted potatoes or other roasted root vegetables.

S E R V E S   4   T O   6

Best substitute greens: Just about anything.

For the dressing

¾	cup olive oil
¼	cup balsamic vinegar
1	tablespoon celery seeds
1	tablespoon crushed coriander seeds
1	teaspoon minced garlic
1	tablespoon sugar
1	to 2 teaspoons dried red pepper flakes

For the salad

2	medium red onions, peeled and cut into rounds ½-inch thick
10	small new potatoes, about the size of golf balls, cooked in boiling water until easily pierced with a fork, about 15 minutes
3	tablespoons olive oil Salt and freshly cracked black pepper to taste
1	head lettuce of your choice—red leaf, green leaf, oak leaf, Boston, or romaine—washed, dried, and torn into salad pieces

1. Prepare a medium-hot fire in your grill.

2. In a small bowl, combine all the dressing ingredients and whisk together well. Set aside.

3. Rub the onion rings and potatoes generously with olive oil, sprinkle with salt and pepper, and grill over a medium-hot fire until golden brown, 2 to 3 minutes for the potatoes and 5 to 7 minutes for the onions. Remove and set aside.

4. In a large bowl, combine the lettuce, potatoes, and onions. Stir the dressing well, add just enough to moisten the ingredients (there will be some dressing left over), toss to coat, and serve.

Red Leaf Lettuce with Grapes, Manchego Cheese, and Garlic Chips

WITH SIMPLE SHERRY VINAIGRETTE

This Spanish-inspired salad was put together by Bridget Batson, who served two years as chef of the Blue Room in Cambridge, Massachusetts. Manchego, a hard cheese made from goat's milk, is the best known of many similar excellent Spanish cheeses; if you can't locate it, substitute another hard cheese like Parmigiano-Reggiano. The combination of green grapes and vinegar, which I particularly like, is inspired by the garlic soup of Andalusia in southern Spain. You might try using this simple vinaigrette as a dipping sauce for duck or grilled fish.

SERVES 4 TO 6

Best substitute greens: Any from Column A, page 18.

For the dressing

- ¾ cup extra-virgin olive oil
- ¼ cup sherry vinegar (or substitute fresh lemon juice)
- 1 tablespoon minced shallots
  Salt and freshly cracked black pepper to taste

For the salad

- ⅓ cup olive oil
- 10 cloves garlic, peeled and thinly sliced
- 1 head red leaf lettuce, any bruised outer leaves removed, remaining leaves washed, dried, and torn into thirds
- ¾ cup seedless green grapes, halved
- ½ pound manchego cheese (or substitute Parmesan cheese), shaved

1. In a small bowl, whisk together all the dressing ingredients.

2. In a small sauté pan, heat the olive oil over medium heat until hot but not smoking. Add the garlic slices and sauté, stirring constantly to prevent burning, until they are light brown, 3 to 4 minutes. Remove and drain on paper towels.

3. In a large bowl, combine the lettuce and grapes. Stir the dressing well, add just enough to moisten the ingredients (you will have some dressing left over), and toss to coat. Place the lettuce and grapes on a large platter or individual serving plates, sprinkle with the cheese and garlic chips, and serve.

4

SALADS FOR THE PERFECT TOMATO

NOTHING BEATS THE TASTE of a vine-ripened August tomato at its peak. The layers of flavor are rich, dense, and intense, perfectly balanced by just a slight undercurrent of acidity, so that you can eat tomato after tomato without feeling overwhelmed.

When you have some of these beauties in the kitchen, it's time to celebrate their arrival, which means pairing them with ingredients that don't overwhelm, but complement them. Sometimes you may want only the tomato, some ultra-fresh basil, and the finest olive oil and vinegar you can get your hands on. Other times you may want to surround the tomato with a larger cast of supporting players, like the parsley, bulgur, and feta cheese that so often accompany it in the Middle East. Or maybe you want to pair it with some smooth pancetta and loamy black olives, or romaine lettuce and some crunchy cornbread croutons.

In this chapter, you will find a handful of salads designed to celebrate and enhance the most perfect tomatoes you can find. And remember, if you don't feel like preparing an entire salad, you can always sprinkle your tomato with a little salt and freshly cracked pepper, drizzle it with any one of the dressings here, and enjoy an easy, fantastic summer treat.

August Tomato and Basil Salad

WITH REALLY EXPENSIVE OIL AND
BALSAMIC VINEGAR

Now's the time to break out that boutique olive oil and aged balsamic vinegar you've been saving, because this is the ultimate tomato salad: rich, meaty tomatoes combined with aromatic basil, fruity olive oil, large-cracked pepper, a bit of salt, and the layered flavors of aged balsamic vinegar. When tomatoes are at their peak, no combination of flavors in the world can beat this. This is my favorite salad with a simple grilled steak.

S E R V E S 4

2 cups loosely packed fresh basil leaves,
washed and dried

4 vine-ripened tomatoes (beefsteak if you can get
them), about the size of baseballs, cored and
cut into slices about 1 inch thick

8 to 12 vine-ripened cherry tomatoes, if available

½ cup top-quality extra-virgin olive oil (see page 35)

3 tablespoons top-quality balsamic vinegar
(see page 40)

¼ cup freshly cracked black pepper
Kosher salt to taste

Cover a platter with the basil, then lay the tomatoes over the top. Sprinkle in succession with the olive oil, vinegar, pepper, and salt. Eat it up.

Boston Lettuce with Tomato and Blue Cheese

WITH SIMPLE BALSAMIC VINAIGRETTE

This perennial classic, whose keys to success are August tomatoes and hyper-fresh lettuce that has been dried well so the dressing can cling to it properly, demonstrates clearly that food doesn't have to be either hard to get or hard to cook in order to taste fantastic. The layers of flavor in a truly vine-ripened tomato range from a rich sweetness to a tart acidity. A good blue cheese has the same type of flavor layering, though mostly in the tangy area. So put them together, and you've got enough flavors going on to keep your taste buds popping with every bite. Maytag blue cheese from Iowa is a good choice here, but you can use any good-quality blue cheese.

S E R V E S   4   T O   6

Best substitute greens: Any from Column A, page 18.

For the dressing

¾ cup extra-virgin olive oil

¼ cup balsamic vinegar

Salt and freshly cracked black pepper to taste

For the salad

1 large head Boston lettuce, any tough outer leaves removed, inner leaves washed, dried, and torn in half

4 medium tomatoes, cored and cut into eighths

6 ounces blue cheese of your choice, crumbled

1. In a small bowl, combine the dressing ingredients and whisk until well blended.

2. Place the lettuce and tomatoes in a large bowl. Stir the dressing well, add just enough to moisten the ingredients (there may be some dressing left over), and toss to coat. Place on a platter or individual serving plates, sprinkle the blue cheese over the top, and serve.

Parsley and Tomato Salad with Bulgur and Feta Cheese

WITH SIMPLE VINAIGRETTE

Parsley is a vastly underrated herb, unfairly relegated by many cooks to the role of garnish. But this fate ignores the single virtue that has placed parsley high on the list of the world's most widely used herbs—its mild, slightly grassy flavor with hints of mint and faint undertones of bitterness. Cooks in the Middle East are well aware of this, and in the great tomato-parsley tradition of that area, here's a salad based on a tabbouleh, but with proportions of the main ingredients reversed and some feta cheese thrown in.

S E R V E S   4   T O   6

For the dressing

- ¾ cup extra-virgin olive oil
- 3 tablespoons fresh lemon juice (about 1 medium lemon)
- 2 tablespoons red wine vinegar
- Salt and freshly cracked black pepper to taste

For the salad

- 2 bunches fresh flat-leaf parsley, stemmed, washed, and dried
- 2 vine-ripened tomatoes about the size of baseballs, cored and diced large
- ¼ cup bulgur, covered with boiling water and allowed to stand for 1 hour
- 8 ounces feta cheese, coarsely crumbled
- ½ cup pitted Kalamata or other briny black olives

1. In a small bowl, combine all the dressing ingredients and whisk them together well.

2. In a large bowl, combine all the salad ingredients. Stir the dressing well, add just enough to lightly coat the ingredients (there will be some dressing left over), toss, and serve.

Fancy Greens with Tomatoes and Grilled Garlic-Herb Bread

WITH EXTRA-VIRGIN OLIVE OIL AND LEMON

When you use the fancy mixture of baby greens known as mesclun, it's best to add just a few other ingredients to allow the delicate flavors of the greens to shine through. Here the greens are combined with some vine-ripened tomatoes, simply dressed with oil and lemon juice, and served with grilled garlic-herb bread. Try different kinds of bread for different tastes—I might go with one of those round, chewy peasant loaves cut into thick slices, or even a sourdough loaf.

S E R V E S 4

Best substitute greens: Any baby greens or seedling turnip or beet greens from your garden.

For the dressing

¾ cup extra-virgin olive oil

¼ cup fresh lemon juice (about 1 large lemon)

Salt and freshly cracked black pepper to taste

For the salad

3 tablespoons butter, softened

1 teaspoon minced garlic

¼ cup roughly chopped fresh basil
(or substitute parsley)

4 thick slices good-quality bread

About 10 ounces mixed fancy
baby greens (mesclun)

4 vine-ripened medium tomatoes, cored and quartered

1. Prepare a medium-hot fire in the grill.

2. In a small bowl, combine the olive oil and lemon juice, whisk until well blended, and season to taste. Set aside.

3. In a small bowl, combine the butter, garlic, and basil and mash together until well blended. Grill the bread over a medium-hot fire until browned, 2 to 3 minutes per side. Remove from the grill, spread with the butter mixture, and cut each piece in half.

4. In a large bowl, combine the baby greens and tomatoes. Mix the dressing well, pour just enough over the greens and tomatoes to moisten (there will be some dressing left over), and toss well. Place on 4 individual serving plates, garnish each plate with a piece of garlic toast, and serve at once.

Romaine, Tomato, and Avocado Salad with Cornbread Croutons

WITH CREAMY CHIPOTLE VINAIGRETTE

If you ever have any leftover cornbread, it makes outstanding croutons. The flavor goes particularly well with other Southwestern ingredients, like avocados and the smoky, earthy heat of chipotle peppers, which are dried, smoked jalapeños. Chipotles can be found dried, but they are easier to use if you buy them canned en adobo, *which means packed in a vinegar-tomato sauce. This dressing has a myriad of possible uses, from a sauce for grilled chicken to a dunk for tortillas to a black bean salad dressing to a finishing sauce for barbecued ribs. In fact, it's impossible to overestimate the versatility of this dressing.*

SERVES 4 TO 6

Best substitute greens: Arugula or any from Column A, page 18.

For the dressing

- 1 cup fresh-squeezed orange juice (about 2 large oranges)
- 1 cup red wine vinegar
- ½ cup mayonnaise, yours or mine (page 41)
- 2 tablespoons minced chipotle pepper
- ¼ cup roughly chopped fresh cilantro
- 2 tablespoons cumin seeds, toasted in a sauté pan over medium heat, shaking, until fragrant, 2 to 3 minutes (or substitute 1 tablespoon ground cumin)
- 3 tablespoons fresh lime juice (about 1½ medium limes)
   Salt and freshly cracked black pepper to taste

For the salad

- 1 head romaine lettuce, tough outer leaves removed, inner leaves washed and dried

2   cups cornbread cubes, in ½-inch pieces, toasted in
    a 350°F. oven until nicely browned, 10 to 12 minutes
2   vine-ripened tomatoes about the size of baseballs,
    cored and diced medium
1   avocado, peeled, pitted, and diced medium
½   small red onion, diced small

1. In a small saucepan, combine the orange juice and vinegar.
Bring the mixture to a boil over high heat, then reduce the heat to
medium-low and simmer vigorously until the liquid is reduced by
two-thirds, 25 to 30 minutes. Remove from the heat, allow to cool
to room temperature, then add the mayonnaise and whisk
together until well blended. Add the remaining dressing
ingredients and whisk together.
2. Tear the lettuce leaves in thirds and put them in a large bowl
along with the cornbread cubes, tomatoes, avocado, and onion.
Stir the dressing well, add just enough to moisten the other
ingredients (there will be some dressing left over), toss to
coat, and serve.

Leaf Lettuce with Tomato, Cucumber, and Feta

WITH GREEK-STYLE DRESSING

"Greek salad" is one of the world's most widely used salad titles, but what does it really mean? Traveling in Greece as a youngster, I discovered that the combination of olive oil, lemon juice, and oregano is what it is all about, along with the crisp vegetables found in the Mediterranean. This dressing is also excellent over chopped toasted stale bread as a kind of Greek bread salad, or as a dressing for grilled eggplant or bell peppers.

S E R V E S   4   T O   6

Best substitute greens: Any from Column A, page 18.

For the dressing

¾   cup olive oil

2   tablespoons fresh lemon juice
(about ½ large lemon)

2   tablespoons red wine vinegar

1   teaspoon minced garlic

1   tablespoon fennel seeds

3   tablespoons roughly chopped fresh oregano
Salt and freshly cracked black pepper to taste

For the salad

1   head green leaf lettuce, any tough outer leaves
discarded, inner leaves washed and dried

2   tomatoes about the size of baseballs, cored and cut
into quarters

½   red bell pepper, seeded, halved, and
diced large

½   green bell pepper, seeded, halved and
diced large

½   small red onion, peeled and diced small

1   cucumber, peeled if you want, diced small

½ cup Kalamata or other briny black olives

½ cup feta cheese

1. In a medium bowl, combine all the dressing ingredients and mix well.

2. Tear or cut the lettuce leaves in half and place them in a large bowl along with the tomatoes, bell peppers, onion, and cucumber. Stir the dressing well, pour enough over the top to moisten the ingredients (there will be some dressing left over), and toss to coat. Sprinkle with the olives, crumble the feta over the top, and serve.

Aromatic Watercress, Tomato, and Herb Salad

WITH GINGER-LEMONGRASS VINAIGRETTE

I really like the combination of garden-ripe tomatoes and whole herb leaves. And since the use of whole herbs is very typical of Asian cuisines, why not combine these simple ingredients with an Asian-style dressing? When preparing the lemongrass, make sure that you use only the tender core that resides inside the bottom third of the stalk; the rest is too fibrous to eat. This dressing would also be great with any cold Asian noodle dish, as a marinade for cucumbers, or as a sauce for cold roast chicken.

S E R V E S   4   T O   6

Best substitute greens: Mizuna or any from Column B-2, page 18.

For the dressing

- ¼ cup sesame oil
- ¼ cup fresh lemon juice (about 1 large lemon)
- ¼ cup white vinegar
- 2 tablespoons fish sauce (optional)
- 1 tablespoon minced fresh ginger
- 4 to 6 dashes Tabasco sauce
- 2 tablespoons minced inner stalk from bottom ⅓ of the stalk of lemongrass
- 1 tablespoon sugar
  Salt and freshly cracked white pepper to taste
  (or substitute black pepper)

For the salad

- 2 bunches watercress, trimmed, washed, and dried
- ½ cup loosely packed whole cilantro leaves
- ¼ cup loosely packed whole mint leaves

2 medium tomatoes, cored and quartered

1 cucumber, peeled if you want, sliced into
   very thin rounds

1. In a medium bowl, combine all the dressing ingredients and whisk until very well blended.

2. In a large bowl, combine the watercress, cilantro, mint, tomato quarters, and cucumber. Stir the dressing well, add just enough to moisten the salad ingredients (there will be some dressing left over), toss to coat, and serve.

P.L.T. Salad with Giant Black Olive Croutons

WITH HERB VINAIGRETTE

Taking off from the classic combination of bacon, lettuce, and tomato, this salad veers off a bit by substituting Italian pancetta for American bacon. The addition of black olives makes this a simple, straightforward, but still interesting salad for brunch or even a late weekend breakfast. Toss this dressing with some orzo and black olives, and you've got yourself a fine pasta salad.

S E R V E S   4   T O   6

Best substitute greens: Any from Column A, page 18.

For the dressing

¾   cup extra-virgin olive oil

¼   cup red wine vinegar

1   teaspoon minced garlic

¼   cup roughly chopped fresh herbs: parsley, basil, sage, or oregano

Salt and freshly cracked black pepper to taste

For the salad

½   cup pitted Kalamata or other briny black olives

¼   cup roughly chopped fresh parsley

1   teaspoon minced garlic

1   tablespoon capers

2   tablespoons olive oil

8   half-inch slices French bread, toasted in a 350°F. oven until crisp, 12 to 15 minutes

1   large head Boston lettuce, any tough outer leaves removed, inner leaves washed and dried

2   large vine-ripened tomatoes, cored and cut into 8 wedges each

12 thin slices pancetta (or substitute bacon), cooked until
crisp, 6 to 8 minutes in a sauté pan over medium heat

1. In a small bowl, combine all dressing ingredients and whisk together well. Set aside.

2. Put the olives, parsley, garlic, capers, and olive oil in a blender or a food processor and puree until smooth. Evenly cover the pieces of toast with the mixture.

3. In a large bowl, combine the lettuce and tomatoes. Stir the dressing well, add just enough to moisten the ingredients (you will have some dressing left over), and toss to coat. Put the dressed lettuce and tomatoes on individual serving plates, crumble some pancetta over each serving, and serve accompanied by black olive croutons.

VEGETABLE SALADS

THE RECIPES IN THIS CHAPTER are for people who like vegetables, but not necessarily for vegetarians. I'm firmly convinced that if you don't put yourself in that category, it is only because you have never had a chance to experience the flavors of vegetables picked at their peak of ripeness, then cooked simply.

In the spring and summer, when you can get your hands on locally grown vegetables with real taste, there's nothing better than combining them with some crisp greens in a flavor-packed salad. With all those good tastes going on in the same dish, there's no way you will feel deprived by the lack of meat or fish in the bowl.

We also manage to sneak some fruit into these recipes, like pears, figs, and tangerines; and here and there you will find a few walnuts, a bit of blue cheese, or a handful of legumes, like black beans or lentils. But whether you choose an earthy dish like Spinach Salad with Peppers, Eggplant, and

Roasted Garlic, a somewhat exotic flavor combination like Southeast Asian–Style Napa Cabbage Slaw, or simply a grouping of ingredients that you might not have thought of yourself, like Oak Leaf Lettuce with Grilled Sweet Potato and Asparagus, these are salads in which the vegetables shine.

Arugula and Warm Grill-Roasted Beet Salad

WITH NICK'S VINAIGRETTE

Nick Zappia, general manager extraordinaire, created this salad in consultation with his fiancée Deanna Briggs, the general manager at Hamersley's Bistro in Boston's South End. This is the kind of simple food Nick and Deanna like to cook at home, when they get a few hours off from their eighty-hour work weeks. If you have baby beet greens, they make an excellent substitute for the arugula here. Large beet greens are too tough to eat raw, but you can always sauté them for a couple of minutes, then toss them with the leftover dressing as a side dish.

S E R V E S   4

Best substitute greens: Baby beet greens or any from Column B-1, page 18.

For the dressing

- ½   cup olive oil
- ¼   cup balsamic vinegar
- 1   tablespoon Dijon mustard
- 1   tablespoon honey
- 2   tablespoons chopped fresh herbs: thyme, rosemary, and/or sage
- 1   squeeze of lemon juice
      Salt and freshly cracked black pepper to taste

For the salad

- 4   large beets, about the size of baseballs
- 4   tablespoons olive oil
      Salt and freshly cracked black pepper to taste
- 1   bunch arugula, trimmed, washed, and dried

continued

1. Preheat the oven to 450°F.

2. In a small bowl, combine all the dressing ingredients and whisk them together well. Set aside.

3. Rub the beets with the oil, sprinkle with salt and pepper, and roast until tender, about 30 minutes. Remove from the oven and, as soon as they are cool enough to handle, peel them and cut them into quarters.

4. In a large bowl, combine the beet quarters and arugula. Mix the dressing well, add enough to just moisten the beets and greens (there may be some dressing left over), toss to coat, and serve warm.

Oak Leaf Lettuce with Grilled Sweet Potato and Asparagus

WITH ORANGE–DILL–SOUR CREAM DRESSING

Sweet potatoes and cashews share a rich earthiness that goes particularly well with the lighter flavors of fresh asparagus and oak leaf lettuce. To add to the mix, we put the sweet potatoes and asparagus over the fire for a few minutes to give them a smoky sear. If you can get hold of both red and green varieties of oak leaf, they make a particularly attractive salad. The creamy dressing is excellent over cold asparagus, too, or as a dip for crudités.

S E R V E S   4   T O   6

Best substitute greens: Any from Column A, page 18.

For the dressing

½ cup sour cream

¼ cup red wine vinegar

¼ cup fresh orange juice (about ½ large orange)

1 tablespoon orange zest (orange part only)

3 tablespoons roughly chopped fresh dill

Salt and freshly cracked black pepper to taste

For the salad

16 asparagus stalks, bottom ¼ snapped off

1 medium sweet potato, peeled and cut into circles about ½-inch thick

¼ cup olive oil

Salt and freshly cracked black pepper

1 head oak leaf lettuce, trimmed, washed, dried, and leaves torn in half

⅓ cup cashews, toasted in a 350°F. oven until browned, about 3 minutes, then roughly chopped

1. Prepare a medium-hot fire in your grill.

2. In a medium bowl, combine all the dressing ingredients and whisk them together well. Set aside.

3. Blanch the asparagus spears in boiling salted water for 3 minutes, then immediately plunge them into ice water to stop the cooking process. Rub the asparagus and the sweet potato slices with olive oil, sprinkle with salt and pepper, and grill over medium-high heat until well browned, 2 to 3 minutes per side for both vegetables.

4. Place the oak leaf lettuce in a large bowl. Stir the dressing well, pour enough over the lettuce to coat (you will have some dressing left over), and toss well. Place the dressed lettuce on a platter or individual serving plates and top with the sweet potatoes and asparagus. Drizzle the vegetables with the remaining dressing, sprinkle with cashews, and serve.

Red Leaf Lettuce with Grilled Figs and Baby Artichokes

WITH CREAMY ROASTED RED PEPPER–ORANGE DRESSING

I usually find baby vegetables more annoying than enticing, but baby artichokes are an exception. Baby artichokes are entirely edible, allowing you to have that rich artichoke taste without dealing with the prickly choke of the mature vegetable. Here they are paired with figs and given a smoky flavor over the grill, matched by the roasted peppers in the dressing. The creamy dressing also makes an excellent sauce for grilled or roasted vegetables and goes well with grilled flavorful fish such as tuna or bluefish.

S E R V E S   4

Best substitute greens: Any from Column A, page 18.

For the dressing

- ½ cup mayonnaise, yours or mine (page 41)
- ¼ cup balsamic vinegar
- ¼ cup freshly squeezed orange juice (about ½ large orange)
- 1 roasted red pepper (see page 42), chopped fine
- ¼ cup roughly chopped fresh basil (or substitute parsley)
  Salt and freshly cracked black pepper to taste

For the salad

- 8 baby artichokes, stem and bottom ¼-inch trimmed off
- 1 tablespoon minced garlic
- 3 tablespoons olive oil
- 6 fresh figs, halved
  Salt and freshly cracked black pepper to taste

1   head red leaf lettuce, outer leaves removed and
     discarded, inner leaves washed, dried,
     and torn in half
1   large tomato, cored and diced large

1. Prepare a medium-hot fire in your grill.

2. In a small bowl, combine all the dressing ingredients and whisk together well. Set aside.

3. Place the artichokes in a medium saucepan, add enough salted water to cover, and bring to a boil over high heat. Reduce the heat to low and simmer until the artichokes are easily pierced with a fork, 12 to 15 minutes. Drain, cool to room temperature, and cut in half lengthwise.

4. In a small bowl, combine the garlic and olive oil, and mix well. Rub the artichoke halves and figs with this mixture, sprinkle with salt and pepper, and thread them alternately onto skewers. Grill over a medium-hot fire until both figs and artichokes are nicely browned, 2 to 3 minutes per side. Remove them from the grill and set aside.

5. In a large bowl, combine the lettuce and tomato. Stir the dressing well, add just enough to moisten the lettuce and tomato (there will be some dressing left over), and toss to coat. Place the salad on a platter or individual serving plates, slide the artichokes and figs off their skewers onto the salad, and serve at once.

Red Leaf Lettuce with Tangerines and Jicama

WITH SWEET RED ONION–CUMIN DRESSING

In this salad, sweet tangerines, crunchy jicama, and crisp red leaf lettuce are tossed with a cumin-spiced dressing anchored by the mellow sweetness of sautéed red onions. If clementine oranges are in season, use them in place of tangerines—they have a similar, sweet taste, with the added advantage of being seedless. The onion-cumin dressing can also convert your standard black bean salad into a much more interesting dish.

SERVES 4 TO 6

Best substitute greens: Any from Column A, page 18.

For the dressing

2 tablespoons vegetable oil

2 red onions about the size of baseballs,
  peeled, halved, and thinly sliced

1 tablespoon minced garlic

¾ cup olive oil

¼ cup red wine vinegar

2 tablespoons fresh lime juice (about 1 medium lime)

1 tablespoon sugar

2 tablespoons cumin seeds, toasted in a sauté pan
  over medium heat, shaking frequently,
  until fragrant, 2 to 3 minutes
  (or substitute 1 tablespoon ground cumin)

¼ cup roughly chopped fresh cilantro
  Salt and freshly cracked black pepper to taste

For the salad

1 large head red leaf lettuce, any tough outer leaves
  removed, inner leaves trimmed, washed,
  dried, and torn in half

2   tangerines, peeled, seeded, and separated
    into sections
1   jicama about the size of a baseball, peeled
    and cut into thin strips
1   red bell pepper, seeded, halved, and cut
    into thin strips

1. In a small sauté pan, heat the vegetable oil over medium-high heat until hot but not smoking. Add the red onions and sauté, stirring constantly, until well browned, 7 to 10 minutes. Add the garlic and cook, stirring, an additional minute. Remove from the heat and puree in a blender or food processor. With the motor still running, add the olive oil in a steady stream. Add the vinegar, lime juice, sugar, cumin, and cilantro and pulse to blend. Season with salt and pepper.

2. In a large bowl, combine the lettuce, tangerines, jicama, and bell pepper. Stir the dressing well, add just enough to moisten the ingredients (there will be some dressing left over), toss to coat, and serve.

Romaine Salad with Goat Cheese and Navy Beans

WITH SPICY CUMIN VINAIGRETTE

This salad comes from the creative mind of Andy Husbands, who was chef at the East Coast Grill for three years. Andy is a student of the history of food, and uses his broad knowledge of culinary history to make interesting combinations. Here he brings a lot of Mediterranean flavors together in an excellent combination. The dressing also makes a nice sauce for cold pork or chicken.

S E R V E S 4 T O 6

Best substitute greens: Any from Column A, page 18.

For the dressing

- 2 tablespoons fresh lime juice (about 1 medium lime)
- 2 tablespoons red wine vinegar
- 2 teaspoons cumin seeds, toasted in a sauté pan over medium heat, shaking frequently, until fragrant, 2 to 3 minutes, then ground (or substitute 1 teaspoon ground cumin)
- 1 teaspoon dried red pepper flakes
- 1 tablespoon roughly chopped fresh cilantro
- ½ tablespoon honey
- 1 tablespoon Dijon mustard
- ½ cup olive oil

  Salt and freshly cracked black pepper to taste

For the salad

- ⅔ cup (about 6 ounces) navy beans, soaked overnight in cold water to cover (or substitute a 15-ounce can of beans)
- 1 head romaine lettuce, tough outer leaves removed, inner leaves washed, dried, and cut into ½-inch strips

2   ripe tomatoes, cored and cut into 8 wedges each

½   cup loosely packed fresh basil leaves

4   ounces goat cheese

1. In a small bowl, combine all the dressing ingredients and whisk together well.

2. Drain the dried beans and place them in a small saucepan with enough cold salted water to cover by about 3 inches. Bring to a boil over high heat, then reduce the heat to low and simmer until the beans are tender but not mushy, 1½ to 2 hours. Drain, rinse with cold water, and allow to cool to room temperature. (If using canned beans, drain and rinse well.)

3. In a large bowl, combine the lettuce, beans, tomatoes, and basil. Stir the dressing well, add just enough to moisten the ingredients (you will have some dressing left over), and toss to coat. Crumble the goat cheese over the top and serve.

Hearts of Romaine with Roasted Beets and Asparagus

WITH THOUSAND ISLAND DRESSING

This is one of those salads that the French call salades composée, *or composed salads, which means that you arrange the ingredients on a plate instead of tossing them together in a bowl. It's a perfect salad for late spring, when the very first small beets and tender young asparagus arrive in the markets or in your garden. This dressing is also great for draping over deviled eggs, or you can thin it with a little lemon juice and convert it to a substitute for tartar sauce with fried seafood.*

S E R V E S 4

Best substitute greens: Any from Column A, page 18.

For the dressing

1   cup mayonnaise, yours or mine (page 41)

2   tablespoons apple cider vinegar

¼   cup catsup

2   tablespoons pickle relish

1   stalk celery, diced fine

2   hard-cooked eggs, diced fine

¼   cup roughly chopped fresh parsley

4   dashes Tabasco sauce

2   dashes Worcestershire sauce

     Salt and freshly cracked black pepper to taste

For the salad

4   small beets, about twice the size of golf balls, trimmed, peeled, and halved

2   tablespoons olive oil

     Salt and freshly cracked black pepper to taste

8   to 12 small asparagus stalks, bottom ¼-inch trimmed off

2   heads romaine lettuce
¼   cup roughly chopped parsley

1. Preheat the oven to 450°F.

2. In a medium bowl, combine all the dressing ingredients and mix well. Set aside.

3. Rub the beet halves with oil, sprinkle with salt and pepper, and roast until tender, about 20 minutes. Remove from the oven and, as soon as they are cool enough to handle, cut each half in half again.

4. Meanwhile, in at least 2 quarts of boiling salted water, blanch the asparagus until it is tender but still crisp, 2 to 3 minutes. Drain, immediately plunge into ice water to stop cooking, and drain again.

5. Remove the outer leaves from the romaine until you reach the tightly furled heart, which should consist of 8 to 10 smaller leaves. (Reserve the outer leaves for use in another salad). Cut the romaine hearts lengthwise into quarters and put 2 quarters on each of 4 plates. Put 2 beet quarters and 2 or 3 stalks of asparagus on each plate.

6. Stir the dressing well, spoon some over each serving, sprinkle with parsley, and serve.

Arugula Salad with Black Beans, Corn, and Avocado

WITH ORANGE-CHILE DRESSING

The best chile pepper to use in this spicy dressing is the one that is most readily available in your area; that way, you can use it repeatedly and get to know it well. This dressing has enough flavor to make an excellent salad when used with nothing but arugula, dandelion greens, or other bitter greens. But with the black beans, corn, and avocado, it makes a salad substantial enough for a vegetarian dinner. Our superagent and pal Doe Coover, who eats often at the Blue Room, always insists on having some of this orange-chile dressing on her grilled pork chops or roast pork loin.

S E R V E S   4   T O   6

Best substitute greens: Any from Column B-1, page 18.

For the dressing

- 1 cup freshly squeezed orange juice (about 2 large oranges)
- ¾ cup olive oil
- ¼ cup red wine vinegar
- 1 teaspoon minced garlic
- 1 tablespoon minced fresh chile pepper of your choice
- 2 tablespoons cumin seeds, shaken in a sauté pan over medium heat until fragrant, 2 to 3 minutes (or substitute 1 tablespoon ground cumin)
  Salt and freshly cracked black pepper to taste

For the salad

- ⅔ cup (about 4 ounces) uncooked dried black beans (or substitute one 15-ounce can of black beans)
- 2 small bunches arugula, cleaned, washed, and dried

2   ears corn, blanched in boiling salted water for
    2 minutes, drained, and kernels cut off the cob
    (about 1 cup kernels)
2   ripe but firm avocados, peeled, pitted, and
    quartered
½   small red onion, peeled and thinly sliced

1. In a small saucepan, bring the orange juice to a boil over high
heat, then reduce the heat to medium-low and simmer vigorously
until the orange juice is reduced by two-thirds, 15 to 20 minutes.
2. In a small bowl, combine the reduced orange juice with all the
remaining dressing ingredients, mix well, and set aside.
3. Place the dried beans in a small saucepan with enough salted
water to cover them by about 2 inches and bring to a boil over
high heat. Reduce the heat to low and simmer until the beans are
tender but not mushy, about 1½ hours. Drain the beans and allow
them to cool to room temperature; you should have about 2 cups
cooked beans. (If using canned beans, rinse well and drain.)
4. In a large bowl, combine the beans with the arugula, corn,
avocados, and red onion. Stir the dressing well, add just enough
to moisten the ingredients (you will have some dressing left over),
toss well, and serve.

Arugula Salad with Grilled Fennel and Fried Garlic

WITH CAPER-FENNEL VINAIGRETTE

A multilayered salad, with crunchy garlic chips, smoke-tinged fennel, and capers, this works with the extra-virgin olive oil to produce an intense flavor dynamic. If you are a big fennel fan, consider using two bulbs here, particularly since a few minutes on the grill seems to intensify the vegetable's faint licorice flavor. The vinaigrette is excellent over a grilled oily fish like mackerel or bluefish.

S E R V E S   4   T O   6

Best substitute greens: Any from Column A, page 18.

For the dressing

½   cup plus ⅓ cup extra-virgin olive oil

¼   cup fresh lemon juice (about 1 large lemon)

1   tablespoon fennel seeds

5   cloves garlic, peeled and sliced as thin as possible

⅓   cup large capers, drained and dried
    Salt and freshly cracked black pepper to taste

For the salad

1   large bulb fennel, fronds and bottom ¼-inch
    trimmed off, remaining bulb sliced vertically into
    slices about 1 inch thick

¼   cup olive oil
    Salt and freshly cracked black pepper to taste

1   bunch arugula, trimmed, washed, and dried

2   medium tomatoes, cored and quartered

2   ears corn, blanched in boiling salted water for
    2 minutes, drained, and kernels cut off the cob
    (about 1 cup kernels)

1. Prepare a medium-hot fire in your grill.

2. In a small bowl, combine the ½ cup olive oil with the lemon juice and fennel seeds, whisk to blend, and set aside.

3. In a small sauté pan, heat the remaining ⅓ cup olive oil over medium-high heat until hot but not smoking. Add the garlic slices and sauté, stirring, until just golden brown, 3 to 4 minutes. Remove with a slotted spoon and place on paper towels to dry. Add the capers to the oil in the pan and sauté, stirring, until just crisp, 4 to 5 minutes. Remove with a slotted spoon and place on paper towels to dry. Remove the pan from the heat, allow the oil remaining in the pan to cool to room temperature, then whisk into the olive oil-lemon-fennel seed mixture. Season to taste with salt and pepper and set aside.

4. Rub the fennel slices with the olive oil and sprinkle with salt and pepper. Place on the grill over a medium-hot fire and grill until lightly browned, 4 to 5 minutes per side. Remove from the grill and place in a large bowl.

5. Add the arugula, tomatoes, and corn to the large bowl with the fennel. Stir the dressing well, pour on just enough to moisten the ingredients (you will have some dressing left over), and toss to coat. Place the dressed salad on a platter or individual serving plates, sprinkle with the fried capers and garlic, and serve.

Arugula Salad with Fried Green Tomatoes

AND SWEET CORN DRESSING

When that bumper tomato crop arrives in August and you want to start using some of them while they are still green, fry them in cornmeal and turn them into a light summer salad. This sweetish dressing is also excellent spooned over cold boiled potatoes or tossed with green beans.

S E R V E S   4   T O   6

Best substitute greens: Romaine lettuce or any greens from Column B-1, page 18.

For the dressing

1   ear corn, blanched in boiling salted water for 2 minutes, drained, and kernels cut off the cob (about ½ cup kernels)

2   tablespoons sweet pickle relish

¾   cup olive oil

⅓   cup red wine vinegar

2   tablespoons celery seeds

⅓   cup finely diced celery

Salt and freshly cracked black pepper to taste

For the salad

¾   cup yellow cornmeal

1   tablespoon paprika

Salt and freshly cracked black pepper to taste

2   green tomatoes about the size of baseballs, cored and cut into slices about ½-inch thick

¼   cup olive oil

2   bunches arugula, trimmed, washed, and dried

1. Put the corn and relish in a blender or food processor and puree. With the motor still running, add the olive oil in a steady stream. Turn off the motor, add the vinegar and celery seeds, and pulse to combine. Remove from the blender or food processor, stir in the celery, and season with salt and pepper. Set aside.

2. In a small bowl, combine the cornmeal, paprika, and salt and pepper to taste and mix well. Dredge the tomato slices in this mixture, turning to coat on both sides and shaking off any excess.

3. In a large sauté pan, heat the olive oil over medium-high heat until hot but not smoking. Add a single layer of tomato slices and fry until they are crisp on the outside and golden brown, about 2 minutes per side. Remove, place on paper towels, and repeat with remaining tomato slices.

4. Put the arugula in a large bowl, stir the dressing well, pour just enough over the arugula to moisten (there will be some dressing left over), and toss to coat. Place the dressed arugula on a large platter or individual serving plates, top with the fried green tomatoes, spoon the remaining dressing over the tomatoes, and serve.

Spinach Salad with Peppers, Eggplant, and Roasted Garlic

WITH BASIL VINAIGRETTE

This salad takes advantage of a simple culinary fact: roasting or grilling vegetables both deepens their inherent flavors and adds new layers of taste complexity. With grilled eggplant, roasted bell peppers, and a whole head of roasted garlic for each person, this salad is rich enough to serve as a satisfying lunch or light supper. Show your guests how to squeeze the roasted garlic out onto the toast, and provide plenty of napkins to clean up after the process.

S E R V E S   4

Best substitute greens: Arugula, frisée, or any green from Column C, page 19.

For the dressing

- ¾ cup extra-virgin olive oil
- ¼ cup balsamic vinegar
- 1 teaspoon minced garlic
- ¼ cup roughly chopped fresh basil
- Salt and freshly cracked black pepper to taste

For the salad

- 4 heads garlic, not peeled
- 2 small or 1 large eggplant, cut into rounds about 1½ inches thick
- ½ cup olive oil
- Salt and freshly cracked black pepper to taste
- About 10 ounces spinach, trimmed, washed, and dried
- 4 roasted red or yellow bell peppers (page 42), seeded and cut into thin strips
- 4 slices good-quality bread, toasted

1. Prepare a medium fire in your grill. Preheat the oven to 300°F.
2. In a small bowl, combine all the dressing ingredients and whisk together well. Set aside.
3. Slice the top ¼-inch off the heads of garlic and place the heads in the middle of a foot-long sheet of aluminum foil. Pour ¼ cup of the olive oil over the top of the bulbs, then wrap them up tightly. Place in oven and roast for about 1 hour, or until the individual garlic cloves are soft to the touch.
4. Meanwhile, rub the eggplant rounds with remaining olive oil, sprinkle with salt and pepper, and grill over a medium fire until they are well browned outside and soft inside, 2 to 3 minutes per side. Remove from the heat and, as soon as they are cool enough to handle, cut each round into quarters.
5. In a large bowl, combine the spinach, roasted peppers, and eggplant. Stir the dressing well, add just enough to moisten the ingredients (there will be some dressing left over), and toss to coat. Place on individual plates, put a head of roasted garlic and a slice of toast on each plate, and serve.

Spinach and Lentil Salad with Toasted Walnuts

AND CHILE-BEET DRESSING

This is a case of earthy flavor matching earthy flavor: the beets in the spicy, flavorful dressing go up against the lentils and walnuts in the salad. Toasting the walnuts releases their aromatic oils, which greatly increases their flavor. If you have a cast-iron skillet, that's best for toasting these nuts. The chili-beet dressing is almost like a relish, nice and chunky with lots of flavor. Its strength matches up really well with cold leftover grilled meat.

S E R V E S   4   T O   6

Best substitute greens: Romaine lettuce or any green from Column C, page 19.

For the dressing

- ¾ cup olive oil
- ¼ cup red wine vinegar
- 2 medium beets, larger than golf balls but smaller than baseballs, boiled in salted water to cover until tender, 40 to 50 minutes, then trimmed, peeled, and diced fine
- ¼ cup roughly chopped fresh cilantro
- 2 tablespoons minced fresh chile pepper of your choice
- 1 teaspoon minced garlic
- 1 tablespoon cumin seeds, toasted in a sauté pan over medium heat, shaking frequently, until fragrant, 2 to 3 minutes (or substitute 1½ teaspoons ground cumin)
- 1 tablespoon cracked coriander seeds (or substitute 2 teaspoons ground coriander) Salt and freshly cracked black pepper to taste

For the salad

½   cup lentils of your choice, well washed
     and picked over

1   teaspoon salt
     About 10 ounces spinach, trimmed,
     washed, and dried

1   medium carrot, peeled and cut into thin rounds

½   cup walnuts, toasted in a cast-iron skillet or sauté
     pan until fragrant, about 5 minutes, then roughly
     chopped

1. In a medium bowl, combine all the dressing ingredients and mix well. Set aside.

2. Place the lentils and salt in a small saucepan, add enough water to cover by about 1½ inches, and bring to a boil over high heat. Reduce the heat to low and simmer, uncovered, until the lentils are tender but still firm, about 25 minutes. Drain and allow to cool to room temperature.

3. In a large bowl, combine the lentils, spinach, and carrot. Stir the dressing well, add enough to moisten the ingredients (there may be some dressing left over), and toss to coat. Place the salad on a platter or individual serving plates, sprinkle with toasted walnuts, and serve.

Spinach Salad with Spicy Yellow Split Peas

WITH CHUNKY CUCUMBER-MINT DRESSING

For this Indian-inspired salad, you can use either tender, flat-leafed young spinach or the dark green, crinkly mature type. Either works well with the chile-laced split peas and the creamy, aromatic dressing. If split peas aren't available or if you forget to soak them and it's time to make the salad, you can substitute the kernels from two small ears of corn, reduce the amount of chile pepper by half, and not bother with the simmering. The cucumber-mint dressing, which is kind of like a thin version of the Indian condiment raita, also makes a good cooling accompaniment to any spicy hot dish.

S E R V E S   4   T O   6

Best substitute greens: Baby amaranth greens if you can find them, or any green from Column C, page 19.

For the dressing

- ¼ cup plain yogurt
- ¼ cup chutney of your choice
- ½ cucumber, peeled and seeded
- ¼ cup olive oil
- ¼ cup red wine vinegar
- 1 tablespoon curry powder
- ¼ cup chopped fresh mint
  Salt and freshly cracked black pepper to taste

For the salad

- 2 tablespoons vegetable oil
- 1 small red onion, peeled, halved, and thinly sliced
- 2 tablespoons minced fresh chile pepper of your choice
- ⅓ cup yellow split peas, picked over and soaked for 2 hours in cold water to cover

1½ cups water

Salt and freshly cracked black pepper to taste

1   10-ounce package mature spinach or 2 small bunches
    young spinach, trimmed, washed, and dried

1   large tomato, cored and diced large

1. In a blender or food processor, combine the yogurt, chutney, and cucumber and blend well. With the motor still running, add the olive oil in a steady stream. Turn the motor off, add the red wine vinegar, curry powder, and mint, pulse to blend, and season with salt and pepper. Set aside.

2. In a small saucepan, heat the oil over medium-high heat until hot but not smoking. Add the onion and sauté, stirring occasionally, until transparent, 5 to 7 minutes. Add the chile and split peas, and sauté, stirring, for 3 minutes. Add the water and bring to a boil. Reduce the heat to low, cover, and cook, stirring occasionally, until the peas are just tender but not mushy, 30 to 35 minutes. Remove the mixture from the heat, season with salt and pepper, and allow to cool to room temperature. (It's okay to refrigerate the peas to speed the cooling process if you want, but if you do, stir occasionally to keep the peas loose.)

3. In a large bowl, combine the spinach, tomato, and split peas. Stir the dressing well, add just enough to moisten the ingredients (there will be some dressing left over), toss to coat, and serve.

Watercress and Endive Salad with Pears and Blue Cheese

WITH ORANGE-BEET DRESSING

Beets not only add an earthy sweetness to salad dressing, they also give the dressing a bright color. Here the slightly sweet dressing is paired with mildly bitter watercress and endive, mellow pears, and tangy blue cheese. This colorful salad makes an excellent first course for a simple meat-and-vegetable dinner, or you can serve it afterward, as a variation on the cheese and fruit dessert. If you enjoy grilling vegetables like fennel or zucchini, this dressing makes a good sauce for them.

S E R V E S   4   T O   6

Best substitute greens: Any from Column B-1, page 18.

For the dressing

1	small beet, larger than a golf ball but smaller than a baseball, cooked in boiling salted water until tender, about 30 minutes
1	cup orange juice (about 2 large oranges)
2	cloves garlic, peeled
1	tablespoon fennel seeds
⅔	cup olive oil
¼	cup red wine vinegar
2	tablespoons fresh lime juice (about 1 medium lime)
¼	cup roughly chopped fresh parsley
	Salt and freshly cracked black pepper to taste

For the salad

2	bunches watercress, trimmed, washed, and dried
1	head endive, cut crosswise into thin rounds
2	ripe pears, cored and cut into thin slices
½	cup crumbled blue cheese of your choice

1. When the cooked beet is cool enough to handle, trim off the ends, peel it, and cut it into quarters. In a small saucepan, combine the beet quarters, orange juice, garlic, and fennel seeds. Bring to a boil over high heat and cook, stirring occasionally, until reduced by two-thirds, about 20 minutes.

2. Pour the beet mixture into a blender or food processor and puree. Add the oil, vinegar, and lime juice, and pulse until well blended. Remove from the blender or food processor, stir in the parsley, and season with salt and pepper.

3. Put the watercress, endive, and pears in a large bowl. Stir the dressing well, pour enough over the salad to moisten all ingredients (there will be some dressing left over), and toss to coat. Place the salad on a platter or individual serving plates, sprinkle the blue cheese over the top, and serve.

Watercress and Radicchio Salad with Beets and Leeks

WITH ORANGE-HORSERADISH DRESSING

This salad includes several cooking processes (reducing the orange juice, cooking the beets, grilling the leeks), but they can all be done more or less simultaneously, so the actual time involved is not that great. If you buy a few extra leeks and throw them on the grill, you can serve them the next day, drizzled with the leftover dressing, as an excellent side dish. Or you might want to try adding some mayonnaise to the dressing, then using it as the dressing for chicken salad.

S E R V E S 4 T O 6

Best substitute greens: Any from Column B-1, page 18.

For the dressing

1	cup orange juice (about 2 large oranges)
½	cup sour cream
¼	cup olive oil
2	tablespoons red wine vinegar
3	tablespoons prepared horseradish
2	tablespoons fennel seeds
	Salt and freshly cracked black pepper to taste

For the salad

2	beets about the size of baseballs, roots trimmed
4	leeks, green portion trimmed off, white portion well washed
2	tablespoons olive oil
	Salt and freshly cracked black pepper to taste
2	bunches watercress, trimmed, washed, and dried
1	head radicchio, cored and sliced into thin strips

1. Prepare a medium fire in your grill.

2. In a small saucepan, bring the orange juice to a boil over high heat, then reduce the heat to medium-low and simmer vigorously until the orange juice is reduced to about ¼ cup, 20 to 25 minutes. Remove from the heat, allow to cool to room temperature, then whisk in the sour cream. Add the oil in a slow stream while whisking, then add the remaining dressing ingredients and whisk together well.

3. Meanwhile, in a small saucepan of boiling salted water, cook the beets until easily pierced by a fork but not mushy, about 30 minutes. Drain, plunge into cold water to stop cooking, drain again, and peel. Cut each beet in half from top to root, then cut each half into thin half-moon slices.

4. Rub the leeks with the oil, sprinkle with salt and pepper, and grill over a medium fire until well browned, 3 to 4 minutes per side. Remove from heat and cut into large dice. (If you don't want to light the grill, you can cook the oiled and seasoned beets in a heavy sauté pan over medium-high heat for about 5 minutes per side, or until nicely seared.)

5. In a large bowl, combine the watercress, radicchio, beets, and leeks. Stir the dressing well, add just enough to moisten the ingredients (there will be some dressing left over), toss to coat, and serve.

Frisée with Apple, Cucumber, and Walnuts

WITH YOGURT-MINT DRESSING

In this Persian cousin of the classic Waldorf salad we use frisée, a chicory with small, tender, delicately lacy leaves, which are somewhat less bitter than other members of the chicory family. If you can't find frisée in your local market, watercress, escarole, or curly endive are all fine substitutes in this salad. Try using the yogurt-mint dressing as a dip with pita bread and fresh tomatoes.

S E R V E S 4

Best substitute greens: Any from Column B-2, page 18.

For the dressing

- ¼ cup plain yogurt
- ½ cup olive oil
- 2 tablespoons fresh lemon juice (about ½ large lemon)
- 2 tablespoons honey
- 1 tablespoon ground coriander
- ¼ cup roughly chopped fresh mint
  Salt and freshly cracked black pepper to taste

For the salad

- 1 head frisée, trimmed, washed, and dried
- 1 cucumber, peeled if you want, diced large
- 1 Granny Smith or other tart apple, cored and diced large
- ¼ cup dark raisins
- ½ cup walnut pieces, toasted in a dry skillet over medium heat, shaking, until they just begin to sizzle, about 5 minutes
- ½ cup pomegranate seeds (optional)

1. In a small bowl, whisk together the yogurt and olive oil. Add all remaining dressing ingredients and whisk to combine.

2. In a large bowl, combine the frisée, cucumber, apple, and raisins. Stir the dressing well, add just enough to moisten the ingredients (you will have some dressing left over), and toss to coat. Place on a serving platter or individual plates, sprinkle with the walnuts and the pomegranate seeds if you have them, and serve.

Southeast Asian–Style Napa Cabbage Slaw

WITH GINGER-SOY VINAIGRETTE

Napa is only one among dozens of varieties of Chinese cabbage, but it's by far the most familiar to Americans. Crisp and juicy, it's an excellent foil for a range of Asian flavors, from ginger to soy to sesame. In this salad, we throw in some spicy roasted peanuts to add crunch and a little hot kick; if you make a large batch, you can use the extras as a snack to put out for the cocktail hour. Also, the ginger-soy dressing is excellent over grilled fish or as a dip for tempura vegetables.

S E R V E S   4   T O   6

Best substitute greens: Any variety of Chinese cabbage or any from Column D, page 19.

For the dressing

- ⅓ cup sesame oil
- ⅓ cup rice wine vinegar
- ½ cup soy sauce
- ¼ cup sugar
- 2 tablespoons minced fresh ginger
- 1 tablespoon minced fresh chile pepper of your choice

  Salt and freshly cracked white pepper to taste

For the salad

- ½ cup unsalted peanuts
- 2 tablespoons Tabasco sauce
- 1 tablespoon vegetable oil
- ½ head napa cabbage, outer leaves removed, inner leaves washed, dried, and cut into thin strips
- 1 cup loosely packed fresh cilantro leaves
- 3 scallions, tops and bottoms trimmed, white and green portions cut into thin strips

1   medium carrot, peeled and cut into very thin strips
1   red bell pepper, seeded, halved, and cut into
    very thin strips

1. Preheat the oven to 350°F.

2. In a small bowl, combine all the dressing ingredients and whisk together well. Set aside.

3. In a small bowl, combine the peanuts, Tabasco, and vegetable oil and mix well. Spread the peanuts on a small, ungreased baking sheet and roast in oven until the peanuts are nicely browned, 12 to 15 minutes. Remove the peanuts from the oven and chop them roughly (putting aside any extra ones that you may have made to use as cocktail snacks).

4. In a large bowl, combine the cabbage, cilantro, scallions, carrot, and red pepper. Stir the dressing well, pour on just enough to moisten the ingredients (there will be some dressing left over), and toss to coat. Garnish with peanuts and serve.

6

SALADS WITH MEAT AND FISH

WHEN I WAS A KID AND MY FAMILY went out to dinner, I liked to order the "Chef's Salad." I never quite understood why it was called that (and still don't because I've seen so many versions over the years), but I figured that maybe it was because this particular combination—usually iceberg lettuce topped with neatly divided sections of cheese cubes, strips of ham, and slices of chicken breast—was what the chefs ate in the kitchen as a quick way of getting a complete meal.

You might think of the salads in this chapter as successors to those chef's salads, but with a different chef at the helm. Each of the recipes here contains some type of meat or fish, along with other ingredients that I think make good flavor and texture combinations. Some are Mediterranean in flavor, like Dr. Hibachi's Spinach Salad with Grilled Lamb, Roasted Peppers, and Garlic Chips; others, like Mixed Cabbage Salad with Poached Shrimp and Hearts of Palm, have a more tropical bent; yet others, like Chicory Salad with Sweet Potato, Bacon, and Lemon-Flavored Crumbs, combine classic American ingredients.

What these salads all have in common is that they take off from the idea presented in that classic chef's salad: combining many tastes and textures in a single dish, with the dressing providing a unifying flavor. And, as always, remember that if you don't have a particular ingredient—even if it's the meat or fish—feel free to substitute or just leave it out. After all, in this case you're the chef, so it's your salad.

Salad of Watercress, Apple, and Ham

WITH CREAMY HORSERADISH DRESSING

I really like horseradish in salad dressings, because it provides a little back-of-the-throat heat along with its distinctive flavor. I particularly like it with ham. In that department, my choice for this salad is a Smithfield or other good-quality country ham, but you can use whatever you have available. This dressing will also add some real flavor to sweet potato salad or a ham sandwich.

S E R V E S 4 T O 6

Best substitute greens: Any from Column B-2, page 18.

For the dressing

½	cup mayonnaise, yours or mine (page 41)
3	tablespoons olive oil
3	tablespoons apple cider vinegar
2	tablespoons sugar
¼	cup catsup
2	tablespoons prepared horseradish
½	cup roughly chopped fresh parsley
6	dashes Tabasco sauce
	Salt and freshly cracked black pepper to taste

For the salad

1	bunch watercress, trimmed, washed, and dried
2	Granny Smith or other tart apples, cored and diced medium
½	cup roughly chopped celery
½	cup diced country ham or other ham of your choice
¼	cup dark raisins
¼	cup pecan pieces, toasted in a 350°F. oven, stirring frequently, until fragrant, 5 to 7 minutes

1. Place the mayonnaise in a medium bowl. Add the olive oil in a steady stream while whisking steadily. Add all the remaining dressing ingredients and whisk to combine. *continued*

2. In a large bowl, combine the watercress, apples, celery, ham, and raisins. Stir the dressing well, add just enough to moisten the ingredients (there will be some dressing left over), and toss to coat. Place on individual plates or a serving platter, sprinkle with the toasted pecans, and serve.

Arugula Salad with Red Snapper Ceviche and Papaya

WITH GREEN HERB DRESSING

"Cooking" fish in lime juice, a practice common in both Latin America and Southeast Asia, results in a fish with an unbeatable fresh flavor. You just have to be sure that you start out with high-quality, fresh fish. If you can't locate snapper for this salad, substitute halibut, ocean perch, striped bass, or mahimahi. And for those of you who are squeamish about eating fish that has not been cooked in the traditional way, leave it out. You'll still have a tasty tropical salad. I also like to pour a bit of this dressing on grilled steak.

S E R V E S   4   T O   6

Best substitute greens: Any from Column B-1, page 18.

For the dressing

- 3   scallions, white parts only, trimmed and roughly chopped
- ½   cup loosely packed fresh cilantro
- ½   cup loosely packed fresh parsley
- 3   cloves garlic, peeled
- ¾   cup olive oil
- ¼   cup red wine vinegar
- 1   tablespoon sugar
     Salt and freshly cracked black pepper to taste

For the salad

- 1 pound red snapper fillets, skin removed
- 1 cup fresh lime juice (about 8 medium limes)
- ⅓ cup white vinegar
- 2 tablespoons minced fresh chile pepper of your choice
- 1 bunch arugula, trimmed, washed, and dried
- 1 papaya, peeled, seeded, and diced large
- 2 small tomatoes, cored and quartered
- 1 cucumber, peeled if you want to, and diced large

1. In a blender or food processor, combine the scallions, cilantro, parsley, and garlic and puree. With the motor still running, add the oil in a steady stream. Turn off the motor, add the vinegar and sugar, pulse to blend, and season with salt and pepper. Set aside.

2. Cut the red snapper fillets into finger-size strips and lay them in a shallow baking dish just large enough to comfortably hold them in one layer. In a small bowl, combine the lime juice, vinegar, and chile, mix well, and pour over the fish. Allow to soak for 4 to 6 hours, turning occasionally to make sure that all the snapper is exposed to the lime juice.

3. In a large bowl, combine the arugula, papaya, tomatoes, and cucumber. Stir the dressing well, add just enough to moisten the ingredients (you will have some dressing left over), and toss to coat. Place the salad on a platter or individual serving plates. Remove the snapper from the marinade and discard the marinade. Lay the snapper strips on top of the dressed salad and serve.

Salad of Arugula, Grilled Lamb, and Lima Beans

WITH ROASTED RED PEPPER DRESSING

The next time you're grilling lamb, throw on some extra and use the leftover meat the next day in this salad. You can also substitute leftover steak in this recipe. If you can't find fresh lima beans, though, use fresh green peas rather than frozen, canned, or dried limas—they just don't have the same buttery flavor as the fresh ones. Incidentally, the next time you're looking for a new way to serve green beans or grilled eggplant, try tossing them with this dressing. I also like this dressing on a ham and cheese sandwich.

S E R V E S   4   T O   6

Best substitute greens: Any from Column B-1, page 18.

For the dressing

2   roasted red peppers (page 42), seeded

¾   cup olive oil

¼   cup balsamic vinegar

2   teaspoons minced garlic

¼   cup finely chopped fresh basil, thyme,
      and/or oregano
      Salt and freshly cracked black pepper to taste

For the salad

1   cup shelled fresh lima beans
      (or substitute fresh peas)

1   bunch arugula, trimmed, washed, and dried

1   large tomato, cored and diced large

1   pound grilled lamb, thinly sliced or diced medium

1. Place the roasted red peppers in a food processor or blender and puree. With the motor still running, add the olive oil in a steady stream. Add the vinegar, garlic, and herbs and pulse to blend. Season with salt and pepper and set aside.

2. In a medium saucepan, bring 2 cups of salted water to a boil. Add the lima beans and cook until they are tender but not mushy, about 13 minutes. (If using peas, blanch in boiling water for just 2 minutes.) Drain, plunge in ice water to stop cooking, drain again, and place in a large bowl.

3. Add the arugula, tomato, and lamb to the large bowl. Stir the dressing well, add just enough to moisten the ingredients (there will be some dressing left over), toss well, and serve.

Arugula Salad with White Beans and Shrimp

WITH BASIL VINAIGRETTE

My good friend and teacher, the jolly Bob Kinkead, is the chef/owner of an outstanding restaurant in Washington, D.C., called Kinkead's. His specialty is seafood, and of the many recipes that I've borrowed from him over the years, this is one of the few I'm going to acknowledge. If you have the grilling fire lit for some other purpose, you can grill the shrimp, following the instructions on page 155, instead of poaching it. This basil vinaigrette is really good in potato salad or just drizzled over straight-from-the-garden tomatoes.

S E R V E S   4   T O   6

Best substitute greens: Romaine lettuce or any green from Column B-1, page 18.

For the dressing

- ¾ cup olive oil
- 2 tablespoons red wine vinegar
- 2 tablespoons balsamic vinegar
- 2 tablespoons fresh lemon juice (about ½ large lemon)
- 2 tablespoons grainy mustard
- 1 teaspoon minced garlic
- ¼ cup finely chopped fresh basil (or substitute parsley, thyme, or oregano)
- 1 teaspoon sugar

  Salt and freshly cracked black pepper to taste

For the salad

- 1 cup (about 6 ounces) cannellini or navy beans, soaked overnight in cold water to cover (or substitute a 15-ounce can of beans)
- ½ pound medium shrimp (8 to 10 shrimp), peeled and deveined

1 bunch arugula, trimmed, washed, and dried

1 red bell pepper, seeded, halved, and diced small

¼ cup pitted and roughly chopped Kalamata or other briny black olives

1 small red onion, peeled and diced small

    Salt and freshly cracked black pepper to taste

1. In a small bowl, combine all the dressing ingredients and whisk to combine well. Set aside.

2. Drain the dried beans and place them in a small saucepan with enough cold salted water to cover by about 3 inches. Bring to a boil over high heat, then reduce the heat to low and simmer until the beans are tender but not mushy, 1½ to 2 hours. Drain, rinse with cold water, and allow to cool to room temperature. (If using canned beans, drain and rinse well.)

3. Meanwhile, in a medium saucepan, bring 3 cups of salted water to a boil over high heat. Reduce the heat to low, add the shrimp, and simmer until just tender, about 3 minutes. Check for doneness by cutting one of the shrimp open; it should be opaque throughout. Drain the shrimp, plunge them into ice water to stop the cooking, then drain again.

4. In a large bowl, combine the shrimp and beans with the arugula, bell pepper, olives, onion, and salt and pepper. Stir the dressing well, add just enough to moisten the ingredients (there will be some dressing left over), toss well, and serve.

Boston Lettuce with Poached Salmon, Peas, and Sweet Potato

WITH NEO-GREEN GODDESS DRESSING

In this salad, sweet potato adds a rich, earthy taste to the time-honored combination of salmon and peas. For a modern version of the classic green goddess dressing, I like equal parts dill, basil, or parsley, but you can mix them up in any proportion that appeals to you, or even use just one of them if that's all you have available. The dressing is good with any kind of salmon dish—or any seafood dish at all.

SERVES 4 TO 6

Best substitute greens: Bibb or any other lettuce from Column A, page 18.

For the dressing

- ½ cup roughly chopped fresh dill, basil, and/or parsley
- 3 cloves garlic, peeled
- 1 tablespoon grainy mustard
- ½ cup plain yogurt
- ⅓ cup olive oil
- 2 tablespoons fresh lemon juice (about ½ large lemon)
   Salt and freshly cracked black pepper to taste

For the salad

- 1 pound salmon fillet
- 1 tablespoon kosher salt
- 2 teaspoons freshly cracked black pepper
- 1 large sweet potato, peeled and diced large
- 1 pound green peas in pod (about 40)
- 1 head Boston lettuce, washed, dried, and leaves torn in half

1. In a blender or food processor, combine the herbs, garlic, mustard, and yogurt and process until well pureed. With the machine still running, add the olive oil in a steady stream. Add the lemon juice and pulse to combine. Season with salt and pepper and set aside.

2. Place the salmon in a deep sauté pan, cover with cold water, add the salt and pepper, and bring to a boil over high heat. As soon as the water begins to boil, remove from the heat. Allow the salmon to sit in the hot water for 30 minutes, then remove from the pan and refrigerate.

3. Meanwhile, bring a medium saucepan of salted water to a boil over high heat. Add the sweet potato cubes and cook until they are easily pierced with a fork but not mushy, 10 to 12 minutes. Remove with a slotted spoon or strainer and immediately plunge into ice water to stop cooking. Add the pea pods to the boiling water, blanch for 2 minutes, drain, and plunge into the bowl of ice water. As soon as the peas are cool, drain off the water, then remove the peas from pods.

4. Put the lettuce, sweet potatoes, and peas in a large bowl. Stir the dressing well, add enough to just moisten the ingredients (there will be some dressing left over), and toss to coat. Place on individual serving plates, loosely crumble some of the salmon over each serving, and serve at once.

Mixed Cabbage Salad with Poached Shrimp and Hearts of Palm

WITH LIMEY AVOCADO DRESSING

With crunchy cabbage, delicate hearts of palm, and tender shrimp, this salad has a lot of different textures as well as flavors going for it. If you add an extra tomato to the dressing, you'll have an excellent salsa dip for tortilla chips. In fact, the limey dressing is modeled after the salsa that our friend Jeff Singleton brought back with him after spending a tranquil three months camping on the beaches of Tulum, on Mexico's Yucatán peninsula.

S E R V E S   4   T O   6

Best substitute greens: Any from Column D, page 19.

For the dressing

1	avocado, peeled, pitted, and diced small
1	medium tomato, cored and diced small
½	small red onion, peeled and diced small
¼	cup olive oil
¾	cup fresh lime juice (about 6 medium limes)
1	tablespoon minced fresh chile pepper of your choice
¼	cup roughly chopped fresh cilantro
2	tablespoons cumin seeds, toasted in a sauté pan over medium heat, shaking frequently, until fragrant, 2 to 3 minutes (or substitute 1 tablespoon ground cumin)
	Salt and freshly cracked black pepper to taste

For the salad

1	pound medium shrimp (16 to 20 shrimp), shell on
1	tablespoon kosher salt
	Salt and freshly cracked black pepper to taste
1	cup thinly sliced green cabbage

1   cup thinly sliced red cabbage
1   10-ounce can hearts of palm, cut crosswise
    into thin circles

1. In a medium bowl, combine all the dressing ingredients and mix well. Set aside.

2. Bring a large pot of water to a boil over high heat. As soon as it comes to a rolling boil, add the shrimp and the salt. Cook for 5 minutes, then remove from the heat and drain. When the shrimp are cool enough to handle, peel, devein, and slice them in half lengthwise.

3. Place the red and green cabbage in a large bowl. Stir the dressing well, pour over the salad, and toss to coat. Place the dressed cabbage on a large platter or on individual serving plates, top with the shrimp and hearts of palm, and serve.

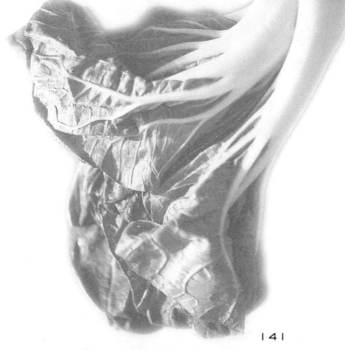

Chef's Salad with Ribs

WITH BARBECUE VINAIGRETTE

Greens and ribs is an old Southern combination and, like a lot of old Southern things, it's still good. Here we put them in the same bowl, instead of just on the same plate. The dressing is outstanding spooned over any roast or grilled beef dish.

S E R V E S   4   T O   6

Best substitute greens: Any from Column B-2, page 18.

For the dressing

- ½   cup of your favorite prepared barbecue sauce
- ¼   cup olive oil
- ¼   cup balsamic vinegar
- ¼   cup roughly chopped fresh basil

For the salad

- ¼   cup ground cumin
- ¼   cup coriander seeds
- 2   tablespoons light or dark brown sugar
- 2   tablespoons salt
- 2   tablespoons freshly cracked black pepper
- 4   pounds baby back ribs
- 2   small bunches arugula, trimmed, washed, and dried

1. Prepare a medium to medium-low fire in your grill. Preheat the oven to 180°F.

2. In a medium bowl, combine all the dressing ingredients and whisk together well. Set aside.

3. In a small bowl, combine the cumin, coriander, sugar, salt, and pepper and mix well. Rub the ribs all over with this mixture. Put the ribs on the grill over a medium to medium-low fire and cook until nicely browned, about 5 minutes per side; you are looking for a beautiful brown exterior. Remove the ribs from the grill, place on a baking sheet, and bake for about 40 minutes. Remove from the oven and slice into individual ribs.

4. Put the arugula in a large bowl. Stir the dressing well, pour just enough on the arugula to moisten (there will be some dressing left over), and toss to coat. Put the dressed arugula on a platter or individual serving plates, top with the ribs, and serve at once.

Mesclun with Roasted Clams and Pancetta

WITH WARM TOMATO-GARLIC DRESSING

Here's to my longtime friend Jimmy Burke, the most talented and inspired chef I ever worked with. The principles he taught me as a young cook have stood the test of time, and still guide my cooking today. The flavors in this wilted salad are also excellent with spinach, and the dressing is also fantastic with pasta or bean salad, or just soaked up with crusty bread.

S E R V E S   4   T O   6

Best substitute greens: Spinach or any mixture of baby greens.

2   tablespoons olive oil

24   littleneck clams, well washed

4   small plum tomatoes, diced small

1   tablespoon minced garlic

⅓   cup fresh lemon juice (about 1½ large lemons)

⅔   cup olive oil

1   cup loosely packed fresh flat-leaf parsley leaves
    Salt and freshly cracked black pepper to taste
    About 1 pound mesclun

½   pound thinly sliced pancetta (or substitute bacon), cooked until crisp, 6 to 8 minutes in a sauté pan over medium heat

1. Preheat the oven to 400°F.

2. In a large, heavy, ovenproof and flameproof pan, heat the oil over high heat until hot but not smoking. Add the clams. As soon as they start to make noise, remove the pan from the stove and put it in the oven. Roast for about 5 minutes, or until the clams are open. Discard any clams that have not opened (be careful, they are mighty hot), and set aside the remaining clams.

3. Put the pan with the clam juice back on the burner over medium heat. Add the tomatoes, garlic, lemon juice, olive oil, parsley, and salt and pepper. Bring mixture just to a simmer, and remove from the heat.

4. Divide the mesclun among the serving plates. Spoon the hot dressing over the greens, divide the clams and pancetta among the serving plates, and serve at once.

Chicory Salad with Sweet Potato, Bacon, and Lemon-Flavored Crumbs

WITH SWEET-SOUR FRENCH DRESSING

One time I ran out of croutons and had nothing left but bread crumbs, so I mixed them with lemon zest and oil, and tossed them into a salad. The flavored crumbs added a nice crunch to the mix. I have always been a huge fan of those Southern classics, sweet potatoes and bacon, so with some of those flavored crumbs and a bit of slightly bitter chicory to cut the richness, it's a salad you could eat all day. You can also brush this dressing on steak or pork chops during the last minute of grilling.

S E R V E S   4   T O   6

Best substitute greens: Any from Column B-2, page 18.

For the dressing

- ¾ cup extra-virgin olive oil
- ¼ cup balsamic vinegar
- 1 teaspoon minced garlic
- 1 tablespoon grainy mustard
- 1 tablespoon sugar
- 2 tablespoons Blue Marlin sauce or steak sauce of your choice
- 1 tablespoon Tabasco sauce
- 1 tablespoon catsup

  Salt and freshly cracked black pepper to taste

For the salad

- ¾ cup homemade bread crumbs
- 1 tablespoon minced garlic
- 3 tablespoons olive oil
- ¼ cup roughly chopped fresh parsley
- 3 tablespoons minced lemon zest

  Salt and freshly cracked black pepper to taste

1 head chicory, trimmed, washed, and dried, and
   leaves torn in half
1 large sweet potato, peeled, diced large, and
   blanched in boiling water until just tender,
   10 to 12 minutes
6 slices bacon, cooked until crispy, 6 to 8 minutes
   in a sauté pan over medium heat, then
   roughly crumbled

1. Preheat the oven to 350°F.

2. In a small bowl, combine all the dressing ingredients and whisk together to blend. Set aside.

3. In a small bowl, combine the bread crumbs, garlic, olive oil, parsley, lemon zest, and salt and pepper and stir to mix well. Toast in the oven until crisp, 5 to 7 minutes.

4. In a large bowl, combine the chicory and sweet potato. Stir the dressing well, add just enough to moisten the ingredients (there will be some dressing left over), and toss to coat. Place on a platter or individual serving plates, top with the crumbled bacon, sprinkle with the flavored bread crumbs, and serve.

Romaine Salad with Crispy Fried Squid
WITH TOMATO-CORN SALSA DRESSING

Squid is a favored food not only all around the Mediterranean but throughout Southeast Asia as well. Over the past few years it has started to become a more popular menu item in the United States. Here the squid is breaded and fried (the most popular way to prepare it in this country), then served with nothing but romaine lettuce and a limey, Mexican-inspired salsa-style dressing that sets up its flavor nicely. Try this salad as a light summer lunch, and try the dressing spooned over roast chicken or grilled pork tenderloin.

S E R V E S   4   T O   6

Best substitute greens: Any from Column A, page 18.

For the dressing

- 1 medium tomato, cored and diced small
- 2 ears corn, blanched in boiling salted water for 2 minutes, drained, and kernels cut off the cob (about 1 cup kernels)
- 1 small red onion, peeled and diced small
- ½ cup roughly chopped fresh cilantro
- 1 tablespoon minced fresh chile pepper of your choice
- ½ cup fresh lime juice (about 4 medium limes)
- ½ cup olive oil
  Salt and freshly cracked black pepper to taste

For the salad

- ¾ cup yellow cornmeal
- ¼ cup all-purpose flour
- 1 teaspoon salt
- 2 teaspoons freshly cracked black pepper
- 1 pound cleaned squid, cut into ½-inch circles
  About 2 cups vegetable oil for frying

1   head romaine lettuce, tough outer leaves removed,
    inner leaves washed, dried, and torn in half

1. In a small bowl, combine all the dressing ingredients and mix
well. Set aside.

2. In a medium bowl, combine the cornmeal, flour, and salt and
pepper and mix well. Dry the squid well and lightly dredge in this
mixture, making sure to coat all sides well, shaking to remove
excess coating.

3. In a small saucepan, heat the oil over medium-high heat until
hot but not smoking (about 350°F.). To check the heat of the oil,
drop a piece of squid into it; the oil should bubble rapidly and
sizzle noisily. Fry the squid in small batches until golden brown, 2
to 3 minutes. Remove and drain on paper towels.

4. Put the romaine on individual serving plates, spoon enough
dressing over the top of each serving to moisten, and top with
some of the squid. Serve at once.

Watercress, Endive, and Radicchio with Smoked Salmon

WITH MUSTARD-HORSERADISH VINAIGRETTE

Although this salad takes just a couple of minutes to prepare, it has a lot of different colors and flavors going on, and makes a great lunch dish. The horseradish is a fairly strong presence in the dressing; I really like it that way, but those who prefer less heat might want to cut the quantity a bit. But if you use the full amount, you can also use the dressing as your shrimp cocktail sauce.

S E R V E S   4   T O   6

Best substitute greens: Any from Column B-2, page 18.

For the dressing

- ¼ cup grainy mustard
- 3 tablespoons prepared horseradish
- ¾ cup olive oil
- ¼ cup fresh lemon juice (about 1 large lemon)
- 1 tablespoon sugar
- ¼ cup roughly chopped fresh parsley
- 2 tablespoons capers
- ½ small red onion, peeled and diced fine
- Salt and freshly cracked black pepper to taste

For the salad

- 1 bunch watercress, trimmed, washed, and dried
- 1 head Belgian endive, outer leaves removed, inner leaves sliced into circles about ½-inch thick
- 1 small head radicchio, tough outer leaves removed, inner leaves cut into thin strips
- 12 ounces smoked salmon, cut into very thin slices
- 2 hard-cooked eggs, roughly chopped (optional)

1. In a medium bowl, combine the mustard and horseradish. Add the oil in a steady stream while whisking. Whisk in the lemon juice, then add all the remaining dressing ingredients and mix well.

2. Put the watercress, endive, and radicchio in a large bowl. Stir the dressing well, add just enough to moisten the ingredients (there will be some dressing left over), and toss to coat. Place on a platter or individual serving plates, lay the salmon slices on top, sprinkle with hard-cooked egg if you want, and serve.

Doctor Hibachi's Spinach Salad with Grilled Lamb, Roasted Peppers, and Garlic Chips

WITH HONEY-SAGE DRESSING

*My high school amigo Ryan Hodges was awarded the nickname Dr. Hibachi
because of the grilling skills he developed during our days of misspent youth.
Ironically, this salad is particularly good for people who for health reasons are
cutting down on red meat but still love the taste. Don't mention that to Ryan,
though, because he ate baby lamb chops the way most people eat oysters—by
the dozen. This sweetish dressing is perfect for drizzling over any lamb dish.*

S E R V E S   4

Best substitute greens: Romaine lettuce or any from
Column C, page 19.

For the dressing

- ½ cup plus 2 tablespoons olive oil
- 4 large cloves garlic, peeled and thinly sliced
- 3 tablespoons balsamic vinegar
- 1 tablespoon fresh lemon juice
- 2 teaspoons honey
- 1½ tablespoons minced fresh sage (or substitute mint)
  Salt and freshly cracked black pepper to taste

For the salad

- 4 small loin or rib lamb chops, each about
  1½ inches thick
  Salt and freshly cracked black pepper to taste
  About 10 ounces spinach, trimmed,
  washed, and dried
- 3 roasted red peppers (see page 42), seeded
  and cut into long, thin strips

1   red onion, peeled, halved, and thinly sliced
¼   cup pine nuts, toasted in a 350°F. oven,
      stirring frequently, until golden, about 10 minutes

1. Prepare a medium-hot fire in your grill.

2. In a small sauté pan, heat the olive oil over medium heat until hot but not smoking. Add the garlic slices and sauté, stirring constantly to prevent burning, until they are light brown, about 2 minutes. Remove the garlic with a slotted spoon and drain on paper towels. Pour the oil into a small bowl and allow to cool to room temperature. Add enough additional oil to make a full ½ cup, then add the vinegar, lemon juice, honey, and sage, mix well, and season with salt and pepper. Set aside.

3. Sprinkle the lamb chops with salt and pepper and grill over a medium-hot fire for 6 to 7 minutes for medium-rare; if you like your lamb more well done, continue to grill, checking every couple of minutes, and remove the chops when they are one state of doneness less well done than you want them to be.

4. In a large bowl, combine the spinach, roasted peppers, and onion. Stir the dressing well, add just enough to moisten the ingredients (there will be some dressing left over), and toss to coat. Place the dressed salad on individual serving plates, place a lamb chop on top of each, sprinkle with garlic chips and toasted pine nuts, and serve.

Spinach Salad with Grilled Shrimp and Pineapple

WITH GINGER-SOY DRESSING

I think tender young spinach is a little better than mature spinach in this salad, but you can go either way. If you use the adult strength, be sure to remove the thick center stems. I strongly recommend adding the fish sauce to the dressing, since it gives it a real depth of flavor, but if you don't have it or decide to leave it out, the dressing will still have plenty of flavor. Try the leftover dressing as a dip for Thai spring rolls or raw vegetables.

S E R V E S   4   T O   6

Best substitute greens: Watercress, mizuna, or any lettuce from Column A, page 18.

For the dressing

- ¼ cup olive oil
- ¼ cup sesame oil
- ¼ cup soy sauce
- 2 tablespoons white vinegar
- 2 tablespoons finely minced fresh ginger
- 4 dashes Tabasco sauce
- 2 tablespoons fish sauce (optional)

For the salad

- 1 pound large shrimp (about 12 shrimp), shelled and deveined
- ½ pineapple, peeled, cored, and cut into chunks slightly larger than bite-size
- 1 red bell pepper, seeded and cut into eighths
- 1 medium red onion, peeled and cut into eighths
- ¼ cup vegetable oil

2 tablespoons five-spice powder

Salt and freshly cracked white pepper to taste

(or substitute black pepper)

10 ounces mature spinach or 2 bunches baby spinach, stemmed, washed, and dried

1. Prepare a medium-hot fire in your grill.

2. In a small bowl, combine all the dressing ingredients and whisk to blend well. Set aside.

3. Rub the shrimp, pineapple chunks, bell pepper chunks, and onion with vegetable oil and sprinkle with five-spice powder, salt, and pepper. Thread these ingredients sequentially onto skewers and grill over a medium-hot fire until the shrimp are opaque throughout and the vegetables are seared and tender, 3 to 4 minutes per side. Remove from the heat and allow to cool to room temperature.

4. Place the spinach in a large bowl and slide the grilled shrimp and vegetables off the skewers into the bowl. Stir the dressing well, add just enough to moisten the ingredients (there will be some dressing left over), toss well, and serve.

7

MAIN-COURSE
SALADS

EVERY CULTURE IN THE WORLD HAS some kind of one-dish meal, a single preparation that makes a satisfying lunch or dinner. Most of us are familiar with these dishes in the form of stews. But here are one-dish meals with a healthful bent; each incorporates some type of crisp, healthy greens, and even the ones with meat have a smaller portion than you would eat if meat were at the center of the plate.

This doesn't mean, though, that these are meals you eat only because they're good for you. Far from it. With the proper salad, you can forget the traditional (read boring) plate arrangement of meat-starch-vegetable, and replace it with a complex interplay of tastes and flavors in a single dish that also happens to be healthful.

Any of the salads in this chapter can be a great meal, with enough heft to satisfy a big appetite. Feel like a seafood dinner? Try Arugula with Sautéed Softshell Crabs and Toast Points, or maybe Romaine and Grilled Salmon Salad with Grilled Red Onions.

Looking for a meal that gives you the satisfaction of red meat without making you feel guilty? Go for Spinach Salad with Grilled Lamb and Apricot Skewers or Spicy Cabbage Salad with Chile-Rubbed Flank Steak.

With flavors from mild to wild, these are salads that make a meal. Of course, in line with the easy-going nature of salads, you can also use them as unusual appetizers, serving each person a small portion.

Watercress and Grilled Chicken Salad with Mangoes and Grapes
WITH CURRY-LIME VINAIGRETTE

Chicken breasts make a good foil for robust, tropical flavors. Grilled chicken breasts are joined here by juicy, sweet grapes, musky mangoes, slightly bitter watercress, and a pungent, Indian-inspired dressing. If you have any dressing left over (and you should), save it for the next time you grill chicken or pork, and brush it on during the last minute or so of grilling.

SERVES 4 AS ENTREE
6 TO 8 AS APPETIZER

Best substitute greens: Any from Columns B-1 or B-2, page 18.

For the dressing

- 2 tablespoons curry powder
- ¾ cup olive oil
- 4 tablespoons red wine vinegar
- 3 tablespoons fresh lime juice (about 1½ medium limes)
- 2 teaspoons minced fresh chile pepper of your choice
- Salt and freshly cracked black pepper to taste

For the salad

- 4 boneless, skinless chicken breasts, about 6 ounces each
- Salt and freshly cracked black pepper to taste
- 1 bunch watercress, trimmed, washed, and dried
- 2 mangoes, peeled, pitted, and diced large
- ½ cup seedless green grapes, halved
- 1 red bell pepper, seeded and diced large

continued

1. Prepare a medium-hot fire in your grill.

2. In a small bowl, combine all the dressing ingredients and whisk together to combine. Set aside.**3.** Sprinkle the chicken breasts with salt and pepper and grill over a medium-hot fire until cooked through, 5 to 7 minutes per side. Check for doneness by slicing into one of the breasts to be sure it is opaque throughout. Remove from heat, allow to cool, and slice thinly.

4. In a large bowl, combine the watercress, mangoes, grapes, and bell pepper with the sliced chicken breast. Stir the dressing well, add just enough to moisten the ingredients (there will be some dressing left over), toss well, and serve.

Red Leaf Lettuce with Peppered Tuna, Green Beans, and Olives

WITH CREAMY TARRAGON DRESSING

Here's a good example of a light, vegetable-dominated salad that makes a great meal on a hot summer day. To keep the lettuce fresh and light, dress it with oil and lemon juice, then pass the creamy-style tarragon dressing for guests to use as they wish on the tuna, green beans, and tomatoes. This dressing is also excellent as a tuna salad dressing or served with fried fish of any variety.

SERVES 4 AS ENTREE
6 TO 8 AS APPETIZER

Best substitute greens: Any from Columns A or B-1, page 18.

For the dressing

- 1 cup mayonnaise, yours or mine (page 41)
- 3 tablespoons capers
- 3 tablespoons chopped sweet pickles
- 3 tablespoons chopped fresh tarragon (or substitute parsley)

  Salt and freshly cracked black pepper to taste

For the salad

1   pound very fresh tuna steaks, 1 to 2 inches thick

2   tablespoons vegetable oil

⅓   cup freshly cracked black pepper

     Salt to taste

2   heads red leaf lettuce, trimmed, washed, and dried

6   tablespoons olive oil

2   tablespoons fresh lemon juice (about ½ large lemon)

½   pound green beans, blanched in boiling water for 2 minutes, plunged into ice water to stop cooking, and drained

2   medium tomatoes, cored and cut into eighths

1   cup Kalamata or other briny black olives

1. Prepare a medium-hot fire if grilling the tuna.

2. In a small bowl, combine all the dressing ingredients and mix well. Cover and refrigerate.

3. To grill the tuna, rub with the oil, pepper, and salt and grill for 3 to 4 minutes per side. Remove and set aside. To pan-sear the tuna, rub with the pepper and salt. Heat the oil in a sauté pan over medium-high heat until hot but not smoking. Add the tuna and cook for 3 to 4 minutes per side for medium-rare. Check for doneness by peeking inside; if it is not done to your liking, return to the fire and check every few minutes. Remove and set aside.

4. Place the lettuce in a large bowl. Add the olive oil and lemon juice and toss to coat. Lay the lettuce on a large platter, arrange the green beans, tomatoes, and olives on top of it, crumble the seared tuna over the top, and serve, passing the dressing separately.

Arugula with Sautéed Softshell Crabs and Toast Points

WITH TIDEWATER TARTAR SAUCE

Softshell is not a type of crab, but a stage of development during which the crab's shell is so underdeveloped that it is soft enough to eat. Fortunately for those of us who love to eat them, this happens every spring. Be careful when you put the crabs into the hot oil, because water in the crabs sometimes explodes and causes the oil to spatter all over the place. This tartar sauce is good with any type of fish or as a dip for tempura vegetables.

S E R V E S   4   A S   E N T R E E
6   T O   8   A S   A P P E T I Z E R

Best substitute greens: Any from Column B-2, page 18.

For the tartar sauce

¾   cup mayonnaise, yours or mine (page 41)

¼   cup roughly chopped fresh parsley

2   tablespoons prepared pickle relish

4   dashes Tabasco sauce

2   dashes Worcestershire sauce

      Salt and freshly cracked black pepper to taste

For the vinaigrette

¾   cup extra-virgin olive oil

¼   cup fresh lemon juice (about 1 large lemon)

3   tablespoons celery seeds

1   tablespoon sugar

      Salt and freshly cracked black pepper to taste

For the salad

1   cup all-purpose flour

¼   cup paprika

1   tablespoon cayenne pepper

2   teaspoons salt

2   teaspoons freshly cracked black pepper

8   softshell crabs, cleaned

½   cup vegetable oil

1   large bunch arugula, trimmed, washed, and dried

2   ears corn, blanched in boiling salted water for 2
    minutes, drained, and kernels cut off the cob
    (about 1 cup kernels)

2   medium tomatoes, cored and diced large

4   slices sandwich bread, toasted, then quartered

1   medium lemon, quartered

1. In a small bowl, combine all the tartar sauce ingredients and mix well. Cover and refrigerate until ready to serve.

2. In another small bowl, combine the vinaigrette ingredients and whisk to combine. Set aside.

3. In a large bowl, combine the flour, paprika, cayenne pepper, and salt and pepper and mix well. Gently dredge the crabs in this mixture, coating on all sides and tapping to shake off excess coating.

4. In your largest sauté pan, heat ¼ cup of oil over medium-high heat until hot but not smoking. Add 4 of the crabs and sauté until just browned, 2 to 3 minutes per side. Remove and drain on paper towels. Repeat with remaining ¼ cup of oil and 4 remaining crabs.

5. In a large bowl, combine the arugula, corn, and tomatoes. Stir the vinaigrette well, add just enough to moisten the ingredients (there will be some left over), and toss to coat. Place on individual serving plates, place 1 or 2 crabs on top of each, and serve at once, accompanied by toast points and lemon quarters. Pass the tartar sauce separately.

Arugula Salad with Pepper-Crusted Quail and Pumpernickel Croutons

WITH SWEET-SOUR BACON DRESSING

Quail always seem like a special-occasion dish, maybe because each person gets a whole bird to him or herself. Butterflying these little birds is fairly easy, and when you coat them with pepper and sauté them over high heat, then combine them with some peppery arugula, pumpernickel croutons, and a rich bacon dressing, you've got a hearty hunter-type salad that's suitable for any celebration. If you have dressing left over, it makes an awesome sweet-potato salad.

S E R V E S   4

Best substitute greens: Any from Column B-2, page 18.

For the dressing

- 4 slices bacon, cut into small pieces
- ¼ cup red wine vinegar
- ½ cup olive oil
- 1½ tablespoons sugar
- 2 tablespoons celery seeds

  Salt and freshly cracked black pepper to taste

For the salad

- 1 cup pumpernickel bread cubes, in ½-inch pieces
- ⅓ cup olive oil
- ¼ cup roughly chopped fresh parsley
- 1 teaspoon minced garlic
- 4 quail, butterflied
- 1 tablespoon salt
- ⅓ cup freshly cracked black pepper
- 3 tablespoons vegetable oil
- 1 bunch arugula, trimmed, washed, and dried

1. Preheat the oven to 350°F.

2. In a small sauté pan, sauté the bacon over medium-high heat until crisp, 6 to 8 minutes, and set aside. Drain all the bacon fat from the pan, pour in the vinegar, return pan to the heat, and bring just to a boil, scraping the bottom of the pan to dissolve any bacon drippings in the vinegar. Remove from the heat and add the oil, sugar, and celery seeds; mix well, and season with salt and pepper. Set aside.

3. In a medium bowl, combine the bread cubes, olive oil, parsley, and garlic and toss well. Toast in oven until nicely browned, 12 to 15 minutes. Remove and allow to cool to room temperature.

4. Rub the quail with the salt and pepper. In a large sauté pan, heat the vegetable oil over high heat until hot but not smoking. Put the quail in the pan and sauté until well browned, 3 to 4 minutes per side. Check the quail for doneness by nicking with a sharp knife at the thickest point; if there is any redness, continue to cook until opaque throughout.

5. Place the arugula in a large bowl. Stir the dressing well, add enough just to moisten the arugula (you will have some dressing left over), and toss to coat. Place the dressed arugula on 4 individual serving plates. Top each portion with 1 quail, one-fourth of the bacon, and one-fourth of the croutons, and serve at once.

Watercress and Rice Noodle Salad with Grilled Quail

AND SESAME DRESSING

This recipe is from Mark Hall, chef at the Blue Room. The combination of quail and Asian flavorings might seem a bit odd, but grilled quail is actually a classic Vietnamese dish served to us in little hole-in-the-wall restaurants all over Ho Chi Minh City. The dressing is also good with any Asian noodle dish.

S E R V E S 4

Best substitute greens: Any Chinese cabbage or any green from Columns B-1 or B-2, page 18.

For the dressing

- ¼ cup olive oil
- 1 tablespoon sesame oil
- ¼ cup rice wine vinegar
- 2 tablespoons soy sauce
- 1 teaspoon minced garlic
- 1 teaspoon minced fresh ginger
  Pinch of dried red pepper flakes
  Salt and freshly cracked black pepper to taste

For the salad

- 4 quail, butterflied
  Salt and freshly cracked black pepper to taste
- ¼ cup rice noodles (or substitute any Asian noodle), cooked in a large pot of boiling salted water until al dente, about 4 minutes, and drained
- 1 bunch watercress, trimmed, washed, and dried
- ½ red bell pepper, seeded and cut into long, thin strips
- 3 scallions, trimmed and cut into long, thin strips (green and white parts)
- ½ small carrot, peeled and cut into long, thin strips

1. Prepare a medium-hot fire in your grill.

2. In a small bowl, combine all the dressing ingredients and whisk together. Set aside.

3. Sprinkle the quail with salt and pepper, and grill over a medium-hot fire for 4 to 6 minutes per side. Test for doneness by cutting into one at the thickest point; the birds should be cooked through, but the meat should still have a somewhat pinkish appearance.

4. In a large bowl, combine the noodles, watercress, bell pepper, scallions, and carrot. Stir the dressing well, add just enough to moisten the ingredients (you may have some dressing left over), and toss to coat. Place the salad on 4 individual serving plates, top each with a grilled quail, and serve at once.

Bibb Lettuce with Poached Shrimp, Avocado, and Cornbread Croutons

WITH CHARRED TOMATO-LIME DRESSING

A subtle way to introduce smoky flavor into a salad is to use grilled vegetables as the basis for the dressing. Many cooks are familiar with roasted red peppers employed in this way, but the same technique can be used with other vegetables, like the charred tomato here. This flavorful dressing is also outstanding when drizzled over grilled steak or used in a black bean salad.

SERVES 4 AS ENTREE

6 TO 8 AS APPETIZER

Best substitute green: Boston lettuce or any from Column A, page 18.

For the dressing

1   large tomato, cored and cut into 1-inch slices

2   tablespoons vegetable oil
    Salt and freshly cracked black pepper to taste

1   large clove garlic, peeled

½   cup olive oil

¼   cup fresh lime juice (about 2 medium limes)

¼   cup roughly chopped fresh cilantro

1   tablespoon cumin seeds, toasted in a sauté pan over medium heat, shaking, until fragrant, 2 to 3 minutes (or substitute ½ tablespoon ground cumin)

1   tablespoon coriander seeds, toasted in a sauté pan (with the cumin seed) over medium heat, shaking, until fragrant, 2 to 3 minutes (or substitute ½ tablespoon ground coriander)

For the salad

1½ pounds large shrimp (24 to 30), peeled
     and deveined

2   heads Bibb lettuce, any bruised outer leaves
     removed, remaining leaves washed and dried

2   avocados, peeled, pitted, and quartered

1   3-inch square stale cornbread, cut into 1-inch cubes
     and toasted in a 350°F. oven until browned,
     10 to 12 minutes

1. Prepare a medium-hot fire in your grill.

2. Rub the tomato with the oil, sprinkle with salt and pepper, and grill over a medium fire until well charred, about 3 minutes per side. Remove from the heat and place in a blender or food processor. Add the garlic and puree. With the motor still running, add the olive oil in a steady stream. Add the lime juice, cilantro, and cumin and coriander seeds, pulse to blend, and season with salt and pepper. Set aside.

3. In a large pot of boiling salted water, cook the shrimp until opaque throughout, 3 to 4 minutes. To check for doneness, cut into one of the shrimp to make sure it is no longer translucent at the center. Drain, plunge into cold water to stop cooking, and drain again.

4. In a large bowl, combine the shrimp, lettuce, avocados, and toasted croutons. Stir the dressing well, add just enough to moisten the ingredients (there will be some dressing left over), toss well, and serve.

Spicy Cabbage Salad with Chile-Rubbed Flank Steak

WITH LIME-PEANUT DRESSING

Turn to this salad when you want a quick but dynamic summer meal. In Vietnam, cooks have a tendency to toss whole herb leaves into their dishes, using them almost like greens. It's an easy way to get deep, aromatic flavors into your food, so here we follow that practice. This dressing is also perfect as a dipping sauce for tempura vegetables, fried or grilled shrimp, or those little Vietnamese spring rolls.

SERVES 4 AS ENTREE
6 TO 8 AS APPETIZER

Best substitute greens: Any other Chinese cabbage or any from Column D, page 19.

For the dressing

- ½ cup fresh lime juice (about 2 medium limes)
- 3 tablespoons fish sauce (or substitute vegetable oil)
- 3 tablespoons sugar
- 1 tablespoon minced garlic
- 1 tablespoon minced fresh ginger
- 2 tablespoons finely chopped unsalted roasted peanuts

For the salad

- 2 tablespoons to ¼ cup minced fresh chile peppers of your choice, depending on your taste for heat
- ¼ cup freshly cracked white pepper (or substitute black pepper)
- 3 tablespoons kosher salt
- 2 pounds flank steak or top round
- ½ head napa cabbage, roughly chopped
- 1 red bell pepper, seeded, halved, and cut into thin strips

½ cup loosely packed basil leaves
½ cup loosely packed cilantro (stems okay)
⅓ cup loosely packed mint leaves

1. Prepare a hot fire in your grill.
2. In a small bowl, combine all the dressing ingredients and whisk together well.
3. In a second small bowl, combine the chile pepper, white pepper, and salt and mix well. Rub the steak liberally with this mixture, then grill for 4 to 6 minutes per side, depending on thickness. Check for doneness by nicking the steak at its thickest point. Because of carryover cooking, you should remove the steak from the grill when it is slightly less done than you want it to be when you eat it. Remove the steak from the grill and set aside to cool slightly.
4. In a large bowl, combine the cabbage, bell pepper, basil, cilantro, and mint. Slice the steak crosswise as thin as possible, then cut the slices into bite-size pieces and add them to the cabbage mixture. Stir the dressing well, add just enough to moisten the ingredients (there will be some dressing left over), toss to coat, and serve.

Chicory with Garlic Pork, Pickles, and Black-eyed Peas

WITH CHARRED TOMATO DRESSING

This salad calls for chicory, which in some parts of the country is called curly endive. I think its strong flavor goes particularly well with the earthy taste of black-eyed peas and the garlic- and herb-coated pork in this Southern-inspired recipe. If you can't find chicory, substitute escarole, frisée, dandelion greens, or even radicchio. This dressing is delicious with any pork product—pork chops, sliced pork sandwich—or mixed with black-eyed peas as a vegetarian side salad.

S E R V E S   4   A S   E N T R E E

6   T O   8   A S   A P P E T I Z E R

Best substitute greens: Any from Column B-2, page 18.

For the dressing

- 1 medium tomato, cored and cut into slices 1 inch thick
- 3 cloves garlic, peeled
- ¾ cup olive oil
- ¼ cup red wine vinegar
- 2 tablespoons finely chopped fresh sage
   Salt and freshly cracked black pepper to taste

For the salad

- 2 cups black-eyed peas (or one 15-ounce can)
- 6 cups water
- 1 tablespoon plus 1 teaspoon salt
- 3 tablespoons minced garlic
- ¼ cup roughly chopped fresh parsley
- 1 teaspoon freshly ground black pepper
- 6 tablespoons olive oil
- 4 pork fillets, 6-ounces each, pounded to
   ½-inch thickness
- 1 large head chicory (curly endive), outer leaves discarded, tender inner leaves trimmed, washed, and dried

1 cup bread-and-butter pickles

1 red bell pepper, seeded and diced small

1 small red onion, peeled and diced small

1. Prepare a medium-low fire in your grill.

2. Grill the tomato slices until nicely charred, 6 to 8 minutes per side. Remove from the grill, place in a blender or food processor along with the garlic, and puree. With the motor still running, add the oil in a steady stream. Add the vinegar and sage, and pulse to blend. Season with salt and pepper and set aside. (If using canned peas, rinse and drain well.)

3. In a small saucepan, combine the black-eyed peas, water, and 1 tablespoon of salt and bring to a boil over high heat. Reduce the heat to low and simmer, covered, for 30 to 40 minutes, or until the peas are tender but not mushy. Drain and set aside. (If using canned peas, rinse and drain well.)

4. Meanwhile, in a small bowl, combine the garlic, parsley, remaining 1 teaspoon salt, pepper, and 3 tablespoons of the olive oil and mix well. Rub the pork fillets all over with this mixture.

5. In a large sauté pan, heat the remaining 3 tablespoons of olive oil over medium heat until hot but not smoking. Add the pork fillets and sauté until just cooked through, 2 to 3 minutes per side. To check for doneness, cut into one of the fillets to see if it is cooked to your liking. Remove the fillets from the heat, cool, and cut them into ½-inch cubes.

6. In a large bowl, combine the pork, chicory, pickles, bell pepper, onion, and black-eyed peas. Stir the dressing well, moisten the salad ingredients, toss to coat, and serve.

Leaf Lettuce with Grilled Scallops, Peppers, and Green Olives
WITH ROMESCO VINAIGRETTE

In Catalonia, in northeastern Spain, cooks often serve seafood with romesco, a classic sauce flavored with almonds, garlic, tomatoes, and a bit of chile pepper. Here we borrow those flavors to make a vinaigrette that perfectly sets up the flavor of the grilled scallops in the salad. When grilling the scallops, make sure they get a nice brown exterior that will contrast with the rich, creamy interior.

SERVES 4 AS ENTREE

6 TO 8 AS APPETIZER

Best substitute greens: Any from Column A, page 18.

For the dressing

¼ cup olive oil

3 cloves garlic, peeled

¼ cup blanched almonds

1 tablespoon minced fresh chile pepper of your choice

1 medium tomato, cored and diced large

½ cup extra-virgin olive oil

⅓ cup sherry vinegar (or substitute red wine vinegar)
    Salt and freshly cracked black pepper to taste

For the salad

1½ pounds large sea scallops

1 red bell pepper, seeded
    and cut into 8 large chunks

1 green bell pepper, seeded
    and cut into 8 large chunks

1 medium red onion, peeled
    and cut into 8 large chunks

3 tablespoons olive oil

3 tablespoons roughly chopped fresh basil
    Salt and freshly cracked black pepper to taste

2 heads green or red leaf lettuce, trimmed, washed,
dried, and leaves torn in half

½ cup pitted flavorful green olives such as picholine,
sevillano, or cracked Moroccan

1 medium lemon, quartered (optional)

1. Prepare a medium-hot fire in your grill.

2. In a medium sauté pan, heat the oil over moderate heat until hot but not smoking. Add the whole garlic cloves and sauté, stirring occasionally, until they begin to brown, 2 to 3 minutes. Add the almonds and chiles, and cook, stirring, an additional 2 minutes. Add the tomato and cook, stirring, 1 minute more. Remove to a blender or food processor and puree. With the motor still running, add the oil in a steady stream. Turn the motor off, add the vinegar, and pulse to combine. Season with salt and pepper and set aside.

3. In a large pot of boiling salted water, blanch the scallops for 1 minute. Drain, immediately plunge into iced water to stop cooking, drain again, and place in a large bowl. Add the peppers, onion, olive oil, and basil; sprinkle with salt and pepper and toss well.

4. Thread the scallops, peppers, and onion in turn onto skewers. Grill over a medium-hot fire until the scallops are lightly browned and the vegetables slightly seared, 3 to 4 minutes per side. Remove from the grill.

5. In a large bowl, combine the lettuce and green olives. Stir the dressing well, add just enough to moisten the ingredients (there will be some dressing left over), and toss to coat. Place the lettuce-olive mixture on individual serving plates, top each with a skewer, and serve garnished with a lemon wedge if you want.

Romaine Lettuce with Green Beans, Sausage, and Peppers

WITH CREAMY GARLIC-LEMON VINAIGRETTE

Sausage may seem like an odd salad ingredient, but when you combine it with some crisp romaine lettuce and lightly blanched green beans, then sprinkle the whole with a good cheese, it makes an excellent entree. The vinaigrette used here is very garlicky, which I think goes great with the sausage; if you're not a garlic fancier, though, you may want to use only a single head in the dressing. This dressing also makes an excellent dip for a platter of fresh summer vegetables.

SERVES 4 AS ENTREE
6 TO 8 AS APPETIZER

Best substitute greens: Arugula or any green from Column A, page 18.

For the dressing

Cloves from 2 heads roasted garlic (page 42), cleaned

1 tablespoon Dijon mustard

¾ cup olive oil

¼ cup fresh lemon juice (about 1 large lemon)

2 tablespoons roughly chopped fresh thyme, oregano, or basil

Salt and freshly cracked black pepper to taste

For the salad

1 head romaine lettuce, tough outer leaves removed, inner leaves washed and dried

½ pound green beans, trimmed and blanched for 1 minute in boiling salted water, plunged into ice water, then drained

1 red bell pepper, seeded and diced large

1 green bell pepper, seeded and diced large

1   pound fresh sausage links of your choice
½   cup grated hard cheese, such as Parmesan or
    Romano

1. In a small bowl, combine the garlic, mustard, and olive oil and whisk to combine. Add the lemon juice and herbs, whisk well, and season with salt and pepper. Set aside.

2. In a large bowl, combine the romaine, green beans, and bell peppers.

3. Cook the sausage in a medium sauté pan over medium-high heat until nicely browned and cooked through; about 10 to 12 minutes. (Be sure to cut into one to be certain they are fully cooked.) Remove from the heat and, while still warm, cut into bite-sized pieces and add to the bowl along with all the other ingredients.

4. Stir the dressing well, add just enough to moisten the ingredients (there will be some dressing left over), and toss to coat. Place on a platter or individual serving plates, sprinkle with the cheese, and serve at once.

Romaine and Grilled Salmon Salad with Grilled Red Onions

WITH CHUNKY AVOCADO DRESSING

This dish is particularly easy to prepare because onion rings and salmon fillets both need a medium-hot grilling fire, and both take about the same amount of time to cook. Before you take the salmon off the grill, cut into the center of one of the fillets to make sure it is cooked to your liking. Believe it or not, this dressing is great on a baked sweet potato. It also is an excellent dip for tortilla chips, or slathered on any cold meat sandwich.

SERVES 4 AS ENTREE
6 TO 8 AS APPETIZER

Best substitute greens: Any from Column A, page 18.

For the dressing

- ½ cup olive oil
- ¼ cup fresh lime juice (about 2 medium limes)
- 1 teaspoon minced garlic
- 1 tablespoon minced fresh chile pepper of your choice
- ¼ cup finely chopped fresh cilantro (or substitute parsley)
- 2 avocados, peeled, pitted, and diced small
- 1 medium tomato, cored and diced small
  Salt and freshly cracked black pepper to taste

For the salad

- 4 salmon fillets, 6 ounces each
- 2 red onions, the size of baseballs, peeled and cut into ½-inch-thick rings
- ¼ cup vegetable oil
  Salt and freshly cracked black pepper to taste

¼ cup cumin seeds, toasted in a sauté pan over
  medium heat, shaking frequently, until fragrant,
  2 to 3 minutes
  (or substitute 2 tablespoons ground cumin)

1 head romaine lettuce, tough outer leaves removed,
  inner leaves washed, dried, and torn or cut in thirds

1. Prepare a medium-hot fire in your grill.

2. In a medium bowl, combine the olive oil, lime juice, garlic, chile pepper, and cilantro and whisk together. Add the avocados and tomato, and stir well. Season with salt and pepper and set aside.

3. Rub the salmon and onion rings lightly with oil. Sprinkle both with salt and pepper and rub the salmon all over with the cumin. Grill both onions and salmon over a medium-hot fire until done, about 5 to 6 minutes per side for both. The onions should be well browned and the salmon should be warm throughout.

4. Place the romaine in a large bowl. Stir the dressing well, add just enough to moisten the lettuce (you will have some dressing left over), and toss to coat. Place some of the dressed lettuce on each serving plate, top with some of the salmon and onion rings, and spoon several tablespoons of the remaining dressing on top. Serve at once.

Spinach Salad with Roast Chicken and Peaches

WITH BLACK OLIVE DRESSING

Traditionally, chicken is poached when it is going to be used in a salad, but that's a pretty bland way to prepare fowl. Roasting the bird in the oven makes it much more flavorful and juicy, and that wonderful crispy skin makes for an excellent salad. Here a black olive dressing provides a little earthy piquancy that complements the chicken perfectly. This salad makes a very nice, light, simple dinner. The dressing is also good as a sauce for pasta or potato salad or smeared on grilled bread.

S E R V E S   4   A S   E N T R E E

6   T O   8   A S   A P P E T I Z E R

Best substitute greens: Any from Column C, page 19.

For the dressing

¼ cup pitted Kalamata or other briny black olives

3 cloves garlic, peeled

1 tablespoon grainy mustard

1 tablespoon honey

¾ cup olive oil

¼ cup balsamic vinegar

¼ cup roughly chopped fresh parsley

Salt and freshly cracked black pepper to taste

For the salad

2 whole (double) chicken breasts, skin on and bone in,
16 to 20 ounces each
Salt and freshly cracked black pepper to taste
About 1 pound spinach, stemmed,
washed, and dried

2 peaches, pitted and cut into 8 slices each

1 red bell pepper, seeded, halved crosswise,
and halves cut into very thin strips

1. Preheat the oven to 475°F.

2. In a blender or food processor, combine the olives, garlic, mustard, and honey and puree. With the motor still running, add the olive oil in a steady stream. Turn off the motor, add the vinegar and parsley, pulse to blend, and season with salt and pepper. Set aside.

3. Rub the chickens liberally with salt and pepper and roast for 35 minutes. To check for doneness, cut into the breasts at the thickest point; if you see any redness near the bone, return the chickens to the oven and check again every 5 minutes until the chicken is free of redness. Remove from the oven and allow to cool slightly. When cool enough to handle, use your hands to remove the meat from the bone; it should come off quite easily. Cut the meat into slices about ½-inch thick.

4. In a large bowl, combine the spinach, peaches, and red pepper. Stir the dressing well, add just enough to moisten the ingredients (there will be some dressing left over), and toss to coat. Place the dressed mixture on individual serving plates, portion out the chicken pieces on top of each serving, and serve at once.

Spinach Salad with Grilled Lamb and Apricot Skewers

WITH CREAMY ROASTED GARLIC–PARMESAN DRESSING

This is one of those salads where the greens are dressed but the remaining ingredients are not. There should be plenty of dressing left over to pass in a pitcher, so folks can drizzle it over the grilled lamb and apricots, too, if they want to. You might also try this dressing spooned over a baked potato, tossed with warm pasta, or as a sauce with roast chicken.

S E R V E S   4   A S   E N T R E E

6   T O   8   A S   A P P E T I Z E R

Best substitute greens: Any from Column C, page 19.

For the dressing

Cloves from 1 head roasted garlic
(see page 42), cleaned

½ cup heavy cream

3 tablespoons grated Parmesan cheese

¼ cup olive oil

¼ cup balsamic vinegar

¼ cup chopped fresh herbs: parsley, basil, oregano, and/or thyme, in whatever proportion you want

Salt and freshly cracked black pepper to taste

For the salad

1½ pounds boneless leg of lamb, cut into
1½-inch cubes

4 apricots, pitted and quartered (or substitute peaches)

1 red bell pepper, seeded and cut into 8 large chunks

¼ cup olive oil

Salt and freshly cracked black pepper to taste

About 1 pound spinach, well washed
and dried

1. Prepare a medium-hot fire in your grill.

2. Place the garlic, cream, and Parmesan in a blender or food processor and puree. With the motor still running, add the olive oil in a steady stream. Turn off the motor, add the vinegar and herbs, and pulse to combine. Season to taste with salt and pepper and set aside.

3. Rub the lamb, apricots, and bell pepper lightly with the vegetable oil, sprinkle with salt and pepper, and thread sequentially onto skewers. Grill over a medium-hot fire until the lamb is medium-rare and the apricots and pepper are nicely seared, 3 to 4 minutes per side. Remove from the grill.

4. Place the spinach leaves in a medium bowl. Stir the dressing well, pour just enough over the spinach to coat lightly (there will be some dressing left over), and toss to coat. Put some of the dressed spinach on each plate, top each with some lamb, apricots, and pepper, and serve at once. Pass the remaining dressing for individual use.

8

SALADS WITH EXOTIC FLAVORS

OVER THE PAST FEW YEARS, Americans have gained access to the incredible larder of ingredients and flavors used by cuisines around the world. There is no better way to make use of these intense, deep flavors and exciting new ingredients than in salads.

Some of the recipes here, like the Japanese-inspired Salad of Mizuna and #1 Tuna with Daikon, are combinations of ingredients from a single, somewhat unfamiliar cuisine. Others, like the Salad of Boston Lettuce, Crabmeat, and Mango or the Romaine with Turnips and Pomegranate Seeds, combine the very familiar with the slightly more exotic. Some contain flavors that are exotic not because they are from faraway places but because they are unusual uses of everyday ingredients, like the grilled fruit in our Green Leaf Lettuce with Grilled Peaches and Blue Cheese. Others, such as Escarole with Papayas and Fried Plantains, combine a familiar green with tropical ingredients that have only recently become part of our larder.

In many of these recipes, the more exotic flavors are contained in the dressings, like the Citrus-Chipotle Dressing that uses the flavors of the Yucatán Peninsula, the Middle Eastern–style Yogurt-Coriander Dressing, or the Tamarind-Lime Dressing inspired by a dinner in Malaysia. These dressings are designed to complement the salads in which they are used. Once made, though, they are also ideal for a range of other uses, from dunking vegetables to drizzling over roast chicken or pork to spooning over roasted beets or baked sweet potatoes. With exotic flavors like these, the only limit is your imagination.

Salad of Boston Lettuce, Crabmeat, and Mango

WITH LEMON-LIME DRESSING

The key to this dish is high-quality crabmeat. Some people claim that Dungeness, Jonah, rock, king, or stone crab are the best, but I maintain that the true monarch of crabs is the legendary blue crab. And, as with all seafood, make sure that it is super-fresh. This dressing is also a good match with grilled shrimp or with any kind of seafood.

S E R V E S   4   T O   6

Best substitute greens: Bibb lettuce or any other from Column A, page 18.

For the dressing

- ½ cup olive oil
- 2 tablespoons fresh lemon juice (about ½ large lemon)
- 2 tablespoons fresh lime juice (about 1 medium lime)
- ¼ cup finely chopped fresh parsley
- 4 dashes Tabasco sauce

  Salt and freshly cracked black pepper to taste

For the salad

- 1 head Boston lettuce, washed and dried
- 2 ripe but firm mangoes, peeled, pitted, and diced large
- 1 pound fresh lump crabmeat

1. In a small bowl, combine all the dressing ingredients and whisk together well.

2. In a large bowl, combine the lettuce and mangoes. Stir the dressing well, moisten the ingredients and toss to coat. Place on individual serving plates, crumble the crabmeat on top, and serve.

Arugula and Duck Salad with Mango, Caramelized Onions, and Spiced Pecans

WITH CUMBERLAND VINAIGRETTE

This is a variation on Jasper White's famous duck and papaya salad, which was my favorite dish at his former restaurant in Boston's North End. Keeping the basic sweet and gamey combination intact, I pay homage to the father of the Boston restaurant scene. The dressing borrows the flavors of the classic accompaniment to cold game, Cumberland sauce. This dressing can also be used with any kind of grilled game bird, or even a nice, fat, thick steak.

SERVES 4 TO 6

Best substitute greens: Any from Column B-2, page 18.

For the dressing

½   cup port wine

⅓   cup apricot jam

1   teaspoon minced lime zest (no white)

1   teaspoon minced orange zest (no white)

½   cup olive oil

¼   cup balsamic vinegar

    Salt and freshly cracked black pepper to taste

For the salad

1   tablespoon olive oil

7   dashes Tabasco sauce

½   cup whole pecan halves

4   duck breasts, boneless, about 8 ounces each

    Salt and freshly cracked black pepper to taste

16   pearl onions, peeled

2   bunches arugula, trimmed, washed, and dried

2   mangoes, peeled, pitted, and diced large

1   red bell pepper, seeded and cut into thin strips

1. In a small saucepan, combine the port, apricot jam, and lime and orange zests and cook over medium heat, stirring, until the jam has melted. Increase the heat to high and stir until the mixture starts to boil, then reduce to low and simmer, stirring frequently to prevent burning, until the mixture has been reduced by about two-thirds, about 30 minutes. Remove from heat and allow to cool to room temperature. Add the oil and vinegar, stir to combine, season with salt and pepper, and set aside.

2. Preheat the oven to 350°F.

3. In a small bowl, combine the olive oil and Tabasco, and mix well. Toss the pecans with this mixture, spread on a baking sheet, and toast in oven until nicely browned, 12 to 15 minutes. Remove from the oven and set aside to cool. Keep oven on.

4. Sprinkle the duck breasts with salt and pepper and place in a large sauté pan, fat side down. Cook over medium-high heat until well browned, 4 to 5 minutes per side. Remove from the pan, place on a baking sheet, and roast for 5 minutes for medium-rare. Remove from oven and set aside for 5 minutes.

5. Meanwhile, drain all but about 3 tablespoons of duck fat from the sauté pan, add the pearl onions, and sauté over medium-high heat, stirring frequently, until well browned, 7 to 10 minutes. Remove from the heat and place in a large bowl.

6. Add the arugula, mangoes, and peppers to the bowl with the caramelized onions. Stir the dressing well, add just enough to moisten the ingredients (there will be some dressing left over), and toss to coat. Place on individual serving plates. Slice the duck breast into thin slices and lay them on top of the salads. Sprinkle with the spicy pecans and serve.

Bitter Greens with Fiery Seared Squid
WITH LIME-CHILE VINAIGRETTE

When you cook squid, there are two ways to keep it from ending up with the texture of a wet rubber boot: cook it really slow, or cook it really fast. In this Asian-flavored salad, the squid is seared at high heat, so it is tender and tasty. The key is to have your pan really hot before you put the squid in—but make sure your kitchen fan is going before you start, because if you're doing it right you're going to make some smoke. This dressing would also go very well in a cold Asian noodle salad or as a dipping sauce for grilled asparagus.

S E R V E S   4   T O   6

Best substitute greens: Any from Columns B-1 or B-2, page 18.

For the dressing

¼   cup sesame oil

⅓   cup fresh lime juice (about 1½ medium limes)

¼   cup fish sauce (optional; use olive oil if omitted)

1   teaspoon minced garlic

1   tablespoon minced fresh ginger

1   tablespoon minced fresh chile pepper of your choice

2   tablespoons sugar

For the salad

1   pound cleaned squid, bodies cut into thin circles
     Salt and freshly cracked white pepper to taste
     (or substitute black pepper)

3   tablespoons olive oil

1   tablespoon minced fresh chile pepper
     of your choice
     About 10 ounces mixed bitter greens
     (arugula, watercress, mizuna, tatsoi, radicchio,
     chicory, baby mustard greens, escarole, frisée, or
     dandelion greens), trimmed, washed, and dried

1   small carrot, peeled and cut into very thin strips

1   red bell pepper, peeled and cut into very thin strips

½   cup bean sprouts of your choice (optional)

½   cup unsalted peanuts, toasted and roughly chopped

1. In a small bowl, combine all the dressing ingredients and whisk together well. Set aside.

2. Sprinkle the squid with salt and pepper. In a large sauté pan, heat the olive oil over high heat until the oil just begins to smoke. Add the squid, stir like crazy for 90 seconds, add the chile, and stir for an additional 10 seconds, then remove from the heat.

3. In a large bowl, combine the squid with the greens, carrot, bell pepper, and sprouts. Stir the dressing well, add just enough to moisten the ingredients (there will be some dressing left over), and toss to coat. Sprinkle the salad with the peanuts and serve at once.

Boston Lettuce with Grilled Pork and Pineapple

WITH SWEET AND SPICY GREEN PEPPERCORN DRESSING

It was in Thailand that I first sampled the peppery bite and fantastic flavor of fresh green peppercorns. Since they are hard to get in the United States, I have opted for the dried version here; they have a similar but somewhat less intense flavor. Combined with the dark sweetness of molasses and coriander, they go great with pork. Pass the dressing separately on this one, so people can decide for themselves how much they want. This dressing is also an excellent way to dress up a platter of cold cuts.

S E R V E S   4   T O   6

Best substitute greens: Bibb lettuce, arugula, or any from Column A, page 18.

For the dressing

- 1 cup orange juice (about 2 large oranges)
- ½ cup olive oil
- ¼ cup red wine vinegar
- 3 tablespoons crushed dried green peppercorns
- 1 tablespoon molasses
- 1 tablespoon cracked coriander seeds (or substitute ground coriander)
- ¼ cup roughly chopped fresh cilantro

For the salad

- 1 pound boneless pork loin, cut into 1-inch cubes
- ½ pineapple, peeled, cored, and cut into 1-inch cubes
- 1 red bell pepper, cut into 1-inch cubes
- 1 red onion, peeled and cut into 1-inch cubes
  Salt and freshly cracked black pepper to taste
- 1 head Boston lettuce

1. Prepare a medium-hot fire in your grill.

2. In a small saucepan, bring the orange juice to a boil over high heat, then reduce the heat to medium-low and simmer vigorously until the orange juice is reduced to ¾ cup, 20 to 25 minutes. Remove from heat and allow to cool to room temperature, then add all remaining dressing ingredients and whisk together well. Set aside.

3. Thread the pork, pineapple, bell pepper, and onion onto separate skewers, sprinkle with salt and pepper, and grill over a medium-hot fire for 3 to 4 minutes, flipping over once at the halfway point. The pineapple, pepper, and onion should be nicely seared and a bit softened, and the pork should be just barely pink in the center. To check for doneness, cut into one of the pork cubes and see if it is done to your liking. If you want it more well done, return to the grill and check every couple of minutes. When done to your liking, remove the skewers from the grill.

4. Place the lettuce on a large serving platter. Slide the grilled ingredients off the skewers on top of the lettuce and serve, passing the dressing separately.

Escarole with Papayas and Fried Plantains

WITH TAMARIND-LIME DRESSING

In this salad, a combination of tropical flavors plays against the slight bitterness of escarole. If it's too hot to be in the kitchen frying plantains on the day you make this salad, you can skip them, but they do add an extra tropical dynamic to the dish, particularly if you dip them into the leftover dressing. This slightly sour dressing is also excellent when spooned over a baked potato or some nice grilled pork chops.

S E R V E S   4   T O   6

Best substitute greens: Watercress or any others from Column B-2, page 18.

For the dressing

- 2 teaspoons tamarind paste, dissolved in ¼ cup very hot water (or substitute equal parts fresh lime juice, molasses, and Worcestershire sauce)
- ¾ cup olive oil
- 2 tablespoons fresh lime juice (about 1 medium lime)
- 1 tablespoon molasses
- 1 teaspoon minced garlic
- ¼ cup roughly chopped fresh cilantro
- 1 teaspoon ground allspice

  Salt and freshly cracked black pepper to taste

For the salad

  About 2 cups vegetable oil for deep-frying
- 2 green plantains, each peeled and cut crosswise into 5 pieces

  Salt and freshly cracked black pepper to taste
- 1 head escarole, tough outer leaves removed, remaining leaves washed, dried, and cut or torn into bite-size pieces

1   papaya, peeled, seeded, and diced large
1   cucumber, peeled, seeded, and diced large
1   large tomato, cored and diced large

1. In a small bowl, combine all the dressing ingredients and whisk together well. Set aside.

2. Heat the vegetable oil in a medium saucepan until it is hot but not smoking. (To check the temperature, drop a small piece of plantain into the oil; it should sink to the bottom then immediately start bubbling and rise to the top.) Drop the plantain rounds into the hot oil 3 or 4 at a time and cook until well browned, 2 to 3 minutes. Remove from the oil and drain on paper towels. Next, stand each section of fried plantain upright and, using a frying pan, small cutting board, or whatever else you find to be a convenient squashing tool, squash it as flat as you can. It should have a more or less round shape. Return the flattened plantain rounds to the hot oil, 3 or 4 at a time, and cook until the entire surface is golden brown, about 2 minutes. Remove from oil, drain, season liberally with salt and pepper, and set aside.

3. In a large bowl, combine the escarole, papaya, cucumber, and tomato. Stir the dressing well, add just enough to moisten the ingredients (there will be some dressing left over), and toss to coat. Serve accompanied by plantain rounds.

Hearts of Palm and Cabbage Salad with Avocados and Mangoes

WITH CHILE VINAIGRETTE

Hearts of palm, which really are the center of a palm tree, have a subtle but somehow penetrating flavor that I think matches up nicely with other tropical ingredients. If you can't locate them, though, this salad has enough other flavors to work perfectly well without them. If you don't like too much heat in your food, feel free to cut down on the amount of chile in the dressing. The chile vinaigrette is also nice in an otherwise standard cole slaw or drizzled over grilled corn.

S E R V E S   4   T O   6

Best substitute greens: Any from Column C, page 19.

For the dressing

¾ cup olive oil

3 tablespoons red wine vinegar

3 tablespoons fresh lime juice
(about 1½ medium limes)

2 tablespoons minced fresh chile pepper
of your choice

1 teaspoon minced garlic

¼ cup finely chopped fresh cilantro

1 tablespoon cumin seeds, toasted in a sauté pan,
shaken, until fragrant, 2 to 3 minutes
(or substitute 2 teaspoons ground cumin)
Salt and freshly cracked black pepper to taste

For the salad

2 ripe avocados, peeled, pitted, and quartered

2 ripe mangoes, peeled, pitted, and cut
into large chunks

1 cucumber, peeled if you want to, cut
into large chunks

2   cups shredded red or green cabbage
2   10-ounce cans hearts of palm, drained and cut into
    quarters lengthwise

1. In a small bowl, combine all the dressing ingredients and whisk together well.

2. Place the avocados, mangoes, cucumber, and cabbage in a large bowl. Stir the dressing well, add just enough to moisten the ingredients (there will be some dressing left over), and toss to coat. Place on a serving platter or individual plates, lay the hearts of palm on top, and serve.

Green Leaf Lettuce with Grilled Peaches and Blue Cheese

WITH FAUX CATALINA DRESSING

I know grilled fruit may sound a little funny, but just try it, all right? You will love it, guaranteed. The smoky edge provided by the grilling fire is the perfect complement to the sweet juiciness of summer's fruits. The Catalina dressing is an attempt to duplicate a dressing that I used to enjoy as a child at the Cascades Restaurant in Williamsburg, Virginia. Try it on a chicken or turkey salad. In fact, it's a good all-purpose dressing.

SERVES 4 TO 6

Best substitute greens: Any from Column A, page 18.

For the dressing

2	tablespoons catsup
2	tablespoons grainy mustard
1	tablespoon sugar
1	teaspoon minced garlic
¾	cup olive oil
2	tablespoons lime juice (about 1 medium lime)
¼	cup balsamic vinegar
	Salt and freshly cracked black pepper to taste

For the salad

2	peaches, pitted and halved
2	tablespoons molasses
2	bunches green leaf lettuce, trimmed, washed, and dried
½	cup crumbled blue cheese of your choice

1. Prepare a medium-hot fire in your grill.

2. In a blender or food processor, combine the catsup, mustard, sugar, and garlic, and puree. With the motor still running, add the oil in a steady stream. Turn the motor off, add the lime juice and balsamic vinegar, and pulse to combine. Season with salt and pepper and set aside.

3. Grill the peach halves over a medium-hot fire until just browned, 4 to 5 minutes, brushing with the molasses during the last minute of cooking. Remove from the grill, cut each half into quarters, and place in a large bowl.

4. Add the lettuce to the peaches. Stir the dressing well, add just enough to moisten the ingredients (there will be some dressing left over), and toss to coat. Place on a platter or individual serving plates, sprinkle liberally with the blue cheese, and serve at once.

Salad of Mizuna and #1 Tuna with Daikon

WITH PICKLED GINGER DRESSING

Raw fish and bitter greens make a truly awesome combination—a culinary fact that I confirmed this summer with the striped bass and fluke I pulled out of the Atlantic Ocean waters, then served up raw with arugula from my garden. If you catch the fish yourself, you know that it's fresh; otherwise, find out what fishmonger the Japanese restaurant in your town uses, then tell the merchant you want tuna to use for sashimi. You'll pay more for the fish, but the quality is worth it. If you have some wasabi, you might want to add a couple of tablespoons to the dressing to provide a little extra kick. Try stirring some of the dressing into steamed spinach or kale for an Asian-flavored side dish.

S E R V E S   4   T O   6

Best substitute greens: Any of the Asian greens such as tatsoi, baby mustard, or komatsu, or any green from Column B-2, page 18.

For the dressing

2	tablespoons sesame oil
½	cup olive oil
6	tablespoons rice wine vinegar
¼	cup soy sauce
1	tablespoon sugar
2	tablespoons chopped pickled ginger
1	tablespoon freshly cracked white pepper

For the salad

	About 10 ounces baby mizuna, washed and dried
1	piece pickled daikon about the size of medium carrot, sliced into 12-inch rounds
1	cup hiziki or arame (seaweed)
1	pound #1 tuna, cut into small, thin strips

¼ cup sesame seeds, toasted in a 350°F. oven until
golden, 10 to 12 minutes

1. In a small bowl, combine all the dressing ingredients
and whisk to combine.

2. In a large bowl, combine the mizuna, daikon, hiziki or arame,
and tuna. Stir the dressing well, add just enough to moisten the
ingredients (there will be a bit of dressing left over), and toss to
coat. Place on a platter or individual plates, sprinkle with
sesame seeds, and serve.

Romaine Lettuce with Green Apples and Stuffed Tortillas

WITH CITRUS-CHIPOTLE DRESSING

This salad has a lot of those fantastic Mexican flavors going for it; I find the combination of chiles and green apples to be particularly exceptional. I recommend you use a mild goat cheese to stuff the tortillas because, as my friend Rick Bayless points out in his wonderful book Authentic Mexican, *it has a fresh quality similar to that of Mexican* queso fresco. *If you have dressing left over, use it to dunk chunks of avocado or drizzle it over roast chicken or grilled pork tenderloin.*

S E R V E S   4   T O   6

Best substitute greens: Any from Column A, page 18.

For the dressing

- 1 cup orange juice (about 2 large oranges)
- 2 tablespoons canned chipotle pepper *en adobo*, mashed
- ¾ cup olive oil
- 2 tablespoons red wine vinegar
- 3 tablespoons fresh lime juice (about 1½ medium limes)
- 1 teaspoon minced garlic
- 2 tablespoons chopped fresh oregano (or substitute cilantro)
- 1 tablespoon ground cumin
  Salt and freshly cracked black pepper to taste

For the salad

- 8 ounces mild goat cheese, at room temperature
- ¼ cup roughly chopped fresh cilantro
- 8 corn tortillas

1   head romaine lettuce, tough outer leaves removed,
    inner leaves washed, dried, and torn or cut into
    large pieces
1   Granny Smith or other tart green apple,
    cored and diced large
1   avocado, pitted, peeled, and diced large
1   red bell pepper, seeded and diced large

1. Preheat the oven to 350°F.

2. In a small saucepan, bring the orange juice to a boil over high heat. Reduce heat slightly and boil until the juice has been reduced in volume to about ¼ cup, 20 to 25 minutes. Remove from heat, allow to cool to room temperature, then combine in a small bowl with all the other dressing ingredients and whisk to blend well. Set aside.

3. In a small bowl, combine the goat cheese and cilantro, and mix well. Lay out 4 of the tortillas and spread one-fourth of the cheese-cilantro mixture on each. Top each with another tortilla, place on a baking sheet, and bake until the cheese is melted and the tortillas are slightly browned, 5 to 7 minutes. Remove from the oven and, as soon as they are cool enough to handle, cut each into quarters.

4. In a large bowl, combine the romaine, apple, avocado, and bell pepper. Stir the dressing well, pour in just enough to moisten the ingredients (you will have some dressing left over), and toss to coat. Place the salad on a platter or individual serving plates, arrange the tortilla quarters around the edge of the salad, and serve at once.

Romaine and Tortilla Salad with Avocado

WITH ROAST TOMATO-CHILE DRESSING

Everybody loves tortilla chips, so why not put them in a salad? Actually, this is kind of a Mexican version of the bread salads of Italy and the Middle East. Just be sure that you get the tortilla triangles crispy when you fry them, so they don't become soggy when the salad is dressed. Try putting some of this dressing out on the table for people to dip grilled meats into.

S E R V E S   4   T O   6

Best substitute greens: Any from Column A, page 18.

For the dressing

- 1 medium tomato, cored and quartered
- 1 jalapeño pepper, stemmed
- 2 cloves garlic, peeled
- 2 tablespoons plus ½ cup olive oil
    Salt and freshly cracked black pepper to taste
- ¼ cup red wine vinegar
- 3 tablespoons roughly chopped fresh oregano

For the salad

- ½ cup vegetable oil
- 6 corn tortillas, each cut into 6 triangles
- 1 head romaine lettuce, tough outer leaves discarded, inner leaves washed and dried, then cut into thin strips
- 2 ripe but firm avocados, peeled, pitted, and cut into bite-size chunks
- 1 small red onion, peeled, halved, and sliced very thin

1. Preheat the oven to 450°F.

2. Rub the tomato, jalapeño, and garlic cloves with 2 tablespoons of olive oil, sprinkle with salt and pepper, place in an ungreased roasting pan, and roast until well browned, about 20 minutes. Remove the skins from the garlic, place in a blender or food processor along with the tomato and jalapeño, and puree. With the motor still running, add the remaining ½ cup of olive oil in a steady stream. Turn off the motor, add the vinegar and oregano, and pulse. Season with salt and pepper and set aside.

3. In a medium sauté pan, heat the vegetable oil over medium-high heat until hot but not smoking. Add the tortilla triangles and fry until crisp, 2 to 3 minutes. Remove and drain on paper towels.

4. In a large bowl, combine the tortilla chips, romaine, avocados, and red onion. Stir the dressing well, add just enough to moisten the salad ingredients (there will be some dressing left over), toss to coat, and serve at once.

Romaine with Turnips and Pomegranate Seeds

WITH YOGURT-CORIANDER DRESSING

I love turnips, particularly when combined with Middle Eastern ingredients like pomegranate and yogurt. If you can get your hands on pomegranate molasses it will be worth the effort, because it adds a unique deep, sweet-tart flavor to the dressing. I also like to put this dressing on cold roasted beets or carrots, or on roast beef.

S E R V E S   4   T O   6

Best substitute greens: Any from Column A, page 18.

For the dressing

- ½ cup plain yogurt
- 1 tablespoon pomegranate molasses (optional)
- ¼ cup tomato juice
- 2 tablespoons fresh lemon juice (about ½ large lemon)
- 2 tablespoons coriander seeds, toasted in a sauté pan over medium heat, shaken, until fragrant, 2 to 3 minutes, then cracked
  Salt and freshly cracked black pepper to taste

For the salad

- 1 head romaine lettuce, tough outer leaves discarded, inner leaves washed, dried, and torn in halves or thirds
- 1 cup diced turnip (about 1 small turnip), blanched in boiling salted water until just tender, about 10 minutes
- ½ small cucumber, seeded if you want, diced large
- 1 large tomato, cored and diced large
  Seeds from 1 pomegranate (optional)

1. In a medium bowl, combine all the dressing ingredients and mix well.

2. Place the romaine leaves in a large bowl. Add the turnip, cucumber, and tomato and toss well. Stir the dressing well and pour enough over the salad to just moisten the ingredients (there will be some dressing left over). Toss to coat, place the salad on a platter or individual serving plates, sprinkle with pomegranate seeds, and serve.

Spinach Salad with Mangoes and Potato

WITH CURRY-CHUTNEY DRESSING

If you have a leftover potato from a previous meal, this salad is an ideal way to use it up. Major Grey's is still my number-one bottled chutney, but use whatever version you like best in this dressing. If you happen to have a copy of our book Salsas, Sambals, Chutneys & Chowchows, *K.C.'s Dried Fruit Chutney is great in this dressing. This dressing is particularly good with grilled chicken, or tossed with a bowl of boiled potatoes as a side dish.*

SERVES 4 TO 6

Best substitute greens: Romaine lettuce or any from Column C, page 19.

For the dressing

- ¼ cup prepared chutney of your choice
- ½ cup olive oil
- 3 tablespoons red wine vinegar
- 1 tablespoon curry powder
- ¼ cup chopped fresh cilantro (or substitute mint)
  Salt and freshly cracked black pepper to taste

For the salad

- 1 large white potato, peeled and diced large
  About 10 ounces spinach, trimmed, washed, and dried
- 2 mangoes, peeled, pitted, and diced large
- 1 small tomato, cored and diced large
- 2 tablespoons dark or golden raisins

1. Put the chutney in a blender or food processor and, with the motor running, add the olive oil in a steady stream. Turn off the motor, add the vinegar, curry powder, and cilantro and pulse to blend. Season with salt and pepper and set aside.

2. In a small saucepan of boiling salted water, cook the potato chunks until they are easily pierced by a fork but still offer some resistance, about 8 minutes. Drain, plunge into cold water to stop cooking, and drain again.

3. In a large bowl, combine the potato, spinach, mangoes, and tomato. Stir the dressing well, add just enough to moisten the ingredients (there will be some dressing left over), and toss to coat. Place on a platter or individual serving plates, sprinkle with raisins, and serve.

Watercress with Poached Mussels and Asparagus

WITH ORANGE-SAFFRON DRESSING

I love mussels, and here I combine them with a number of other somewhat delicate flavors. Shortly before you are ready to begin cooking, scrub the mussels under cold water and tear the "beard" off the shell. As I learned from my friend Jasper White, it is easier to do this if you use a cloth towel instead of your bare hands to grab hold of the beard. This is an interesting dressing to use on poached fish, or if you want to make a really high-tone tuna salad.

S E R V E S   4   T O   6

Best substitute greens: Any from Column B-2, page 18.

For the dressing

- ½ cup dry white wine
- ½ cup orange juice (about 1 large orange)
- 1 tablespoon saffron threads, pulverized
- ½ cup mayonnaise, yours or mine (page 41)
- Salt and freshly cracked black pepper to taste

For the salad

- 1 cup dry white wine
- ½ cup water
- ½ cup orange juice (about 1 large orange)
- 1 red onion, peeled and thinly sliced
- 2 garlic cloves, peeled and roughly chopped
- 48 mussels, well scrubbed and beards removed
- 16 asparagus spears, bottoms trimmed off
- 2 small bunches watercress, trimmed, washed, and dried
- 1 red bell pepper, diced medium
- Salt and freshly cracked black pepper to taste

1. In a small saucepan, combine the white wine and orange juice, and bring to a boil over high heat. Reduce the heat slightly and boil until the liquid has been reduced to about ¼ cup, 20 to 25 minutes. About 5 minutes before you take the pan off the heat, stir in the saffron. Remove from heat, allow to cool to room temperature, add the mayonnaise, and stir to blend well. Season with salt and pepper and set aside.

2. In a pot that is large enough to hold all the mussels, combine the white wine, water, orange juice, onion, and garlic. Bring to a boil over high heat, add the mussels, and cover the pot. Allow the mussels to steam until they open, 8 to 10 minutes. Remove from heat and allow to cool until you can handle the mussels without burning your fingers. Strain the juice and save for another use (or discard it if you want), discard any mussels that did not open, and remove the opened mussels from their shells. Set aside.

3. Meanwhile, in a small saucepan, bring about 4 cups of salted water to a boil. Add the asparagus and blanch until tender, 3 to 4 minutes. Drain and immediately plunge into ice water. Drain again and cut each spear into 3 pieces.

4. In a large bowl, combine the watercress, bell pepper, mussels, and asparagus, and sprinkle lightly with salt and pepper. Stir the dressing well, pour on just enough to moisten the ingredients (there will be some dressing left over), toss to coat, and serve.

Yucatán Cabbage Salad
WITH PINEAPPLE-CHIPOTLE DRESSING

This change-up on the old standby, cole slaw, makes use of the flavors of Mexico's Yucatán peninsula—lime, orange, smoky chipotle peppers, and tropical fruit in the form of papaya and pineapple. You can substitute red cabbage or even napa cabbage for the green cabbage if you want. Unlike those made with more perishable greens, this salad will keep for three days, covered and refrigerated. This spicy, highly flavorful dressing is good with any type of pork product—sausage, pork loin, pork chops, or even bacon.

S E R V E S   4   T O   6

Best substitute greens: Any from Column D, page 19.

For the dressing

- 1 cup pineapple juice (or substitute orange juice)
- ¾ cup olive oil
- ¼ cup fresh lime juice (about 2 medium limes)
- 3 tablespoons minced canned chipotle peppers, *en adobo*
- 1 tablespoon minced garlic
  Salt and freshly cracked black pepper to taste

For the salad

- 1 papaya, peeled, seeded, and diced large
- ½ pineapple, peeled, cored, and diced large
- 1 small head green cabbage, cored and cut into thin strips
- ½ cup loosely packed fresh cilantro leaves
- 1 red bell pepper, seeded, halved, and halves cut into thin strips
- ¼ cup cumin seeds, toasted in a sauté pan over medium heat, shaken frequently, for 2 to 3 minutes (optional)

1. In a small saucepan, bring the pineapple juice to a boil over high heat. Reduce heat slightly and boil until the juice has become syrupy, 25 to 30 minutes. Remove from heat, allow to cool to room temperature, then combine with the remaining dressing ingredients and mix well. Set aside.

2. In a large bowl, combine the papaya, pineapple, cabbage, cilantro, and bell pepper. Stir the dressing well, add just enough to moisten the ingredients (there will be some dressing left over), and toss to coat. Sprinkle with toasted cumin seeds if you want and serve.

9

FANCY SALADS

EVERY ONCE IN A WHILE, I get hungry for some truly luxurious food, like a really excellent thick sirloin steak or a serving of lightly seared, incredibly rich foie gras. It's not the kind of stuff I eat every day, but there are times when the expense, the hassle, or the health consequences don't really matter that much. It's what I want, and I'm going to have it.

The salads in this chapter are designed for just those times. Each includes a special-occasion ingredient, from lobster to sweetbreads to high-quality smoked salmon, combined with flavorful greens and other ingredients and tossed with a dressing that complements the whole.

Of course, even if you never get a yen for fancy ingredients these salads can also be used for another purpose—when you want to impress your guests. Whether it's the boss coming over to dinner or a weekend lunch with a potentially

serious romantic interest, any one of these salads
will definitely let that person know that you
consider this a more than ordinary occasion. After
that, the rest is up to you.

Arugula with Lobster and Pancetta
WITH SMOOTH AVOCADO DRESSING

Lobster and bacon are both very rich, but they match up well, particularly with the slight bitterness of arugula to calm them down. Pancetta usually comes rolled up, so when you slice it you get little circles instead of strips. American bacon is also fine in this salad.

S E R V E S   4   T O   6

Best substitute greens: Any from Column B-1, page 18.

For the dressing

- 1 ripe avocado, pitted and peeled
- ¼ cup loosely packed fresh basil leaves
- 1 clove garlic, peeled
- ½ cup olive oil
- 3 tablespoons red wine vinegar
- Salt and freshly cracked black pepper to taste

For the salad

- 6 pieces pancetta (or substitute regular bacon)
- 2 bunches arugula, trimmed, washed, and dried
- 1 red bell pepper, seeded and cut into thin strips
- 8 ounces (about 1 cup) cooked lobster meat, medium diced

1. In a blender or food processor, puree the avocado, basil, and garlic. With the motor still running, add the oil in a steady stream. Turn off the motor, add the vinegar, pulse to blend, and season with salt and pepper.

2. Cook the pancetta, turning once, until it is crispy, 6 to 8 minutes in a sauté pan over medium heat, 10 to 12 minutes in a 350°F. oven. Remove from heat, cool, and crumble.

3. In a large bowl, combine the arugula and red pepper. Stir the dressing well, moisten the ingredients and toss to coat. Place the dressed salad on a platter or individual serving plates, top with the lobster and pancetta, and serve.

Arugula and Seared Sirloin Salad
WITH LEMON-CAPER DRESSING

Nothing beats the taste of a good grilled steak, but these days we are told to cut down on our red-meat consumption for our health's sake. So here's a dish in which you get the taste of steak without the guilt. Using less meat also makes it less expensive, so you can afford a really great piece of steak. The concentrated sweetness of oven-dried tomatoes is particularly good with this salad, and they are very easy to make, but you can also use good-quality fresh plum tomatoes. This simple dressing is a good one to put over baked potatoes or, if you have any of last night's leftover fish, mix it with this dressing for a quick fish salad.

SERVES 4 TO 6

Best substitute greens: Any from Column B-1, page 18.

For the dressing

- 1 tablespoon grainy mustard
- ¾ cup extra-virgin olive oil
- ¼ cup fresh lemon juice (about 1 large lemon)
- 2 tablespoons capers
- ¼ cup finely chopped fresh parsley
- Salt and freshly cracked black pepper to taste

For the salad

- 1 pound high-quality sirloin steak, cut as thick as possible
- Salt and freshly cracked black pepper to taste
- 1 bunch arugula, trimmed, cleaned, and dried
- ½ cup pitted Kalamata or other briny black olives
- 16 dried plum tomato halves (page 41; or substitute 4 halved fresh plum tomatoes)
- About ½ pound good-quality Parmesan cheese

1. Prepare a very hot fire in your grill.

2. In a small bowl, combine the mustard and olive oil, and whisk to blend. Add all the remaining dressing ingredients, whisk together well, and set aside.

3. Sprinkle the steak liberally with salt and pepper and grill over a very hot fire until well seared, 2 to 5 minutes per side, depending on the thickness of the meat. (The steak should be very well seared but still very rare in the middle.) Remove from heat and, when cool enough to handle, slice thinly.

4. In a large bowl, combine the arugula, olives, and tomatoes. Stir the dressing well, add just enough to moisten the ingredients (there will be some dressing left over), and toss to coat. Place the dressed salad on individual serving plates, top each serving with some steak slices, and shave the Parmesan over the top with a vegetable peeler or cheese slicer. Serve at once.

Fancy Baby Greens with Goat Cheese Croutons

WITH SHERRY-HERB VINAIGRETTE

The quickest and easiest way to make this salad is to find a store that sells the mixture of baby greens known as mesclun, from the French word for mixture. This grab bag of tiny greens may include baby oak leaf lettuce, radicchio, mizuna, tatsoi, mustard greens, curly endive, arugula, and perhaps dandelion or chervil. If you've got greens in your garden, pick the seedlings and make your own mixture. If you have leftover dressing, try drizzling it over baby or adult artichokes or some sautéed mushrooms.

S E R V E S   4   T O   6

Best substitute greens: Any edible baby greens, alone or in combination, but the more variety the better.

For the dressing

¾ cup extra-virgin olive oil

¼ cup sherry vinegar (or substitute fresh lemon juice)

1 teaspoon minced garlic

1 tablespoon grainy mustard

2 tablespoons finely chopped fresh thyme, oregano, or marjoram

1 teaspoon sugar

Salt and freshly cracked black pepper to taste

For the salad

About 10 ounces fancy baby greens

12 baguette slices, each about ½-inch thick

1 8-ounce log goat cheese

1. Preheat the oven to 350°F.

2. In a medium bowl, combine all the dressing ingredients and whisk together to blend. Set aside.

3. Toast the baguette slices in oven until crisp, 10 to 12 minutes. Cut the goat cheese into 12 slices and put one slice on each piece of toast.

4. Put the greens in a large bowl. Stir the dressing well, add just enough to moisten the greens (there will be some dressing left over), and toss to coat. Place the dressed greens on individual serving plates, distribute the croutons evenly among the servings, and serve.

Wilted Spinach Salad with Shiitake Mushrooms and Bacon

WITH WARM SHERRY DRESSING

Usually the younger the greens the better, but for this variation on spinach salad mature, dark green, crinkly-leaved spinach is preferred, since it stands up (or wilts down) to the warm dressing better than the young flat-leafed spinach. It may look like there's a lot of preparation here, but it's actually just sautéing a succession of things in a single pan, which takes little effort. I'd also use this dressing over sautéed cabbage.

S E R V E S   4   T O   6

Best substitute greens: Any from Column C, page 19.

For the dressing

6	slices bacon
1	pound shiitake mushrooms, caps only (or substitute any other mushroom of your choice)
1	small red onion, peeled and thinly sliced
1	tablespoon minced garlic
¼	cup sherry
¼	cup red wine vinegar
¾	cup olive oil
1	tablespoon sugar
	Salt and freshly cracked black pepper to taste

For the salad

About 1¼ pounds mature spinach, stemmed, washed, dried, and torn in half

1. In a medium sauté pan over medium heat, cook the bacon until crisp, 6 to 8 minutes. Remove, drain on paper towels, and as soon as it is cool enough to handle, crumble into large pieces.
2. Pour all but ¼ cup of bacon fat out of the pan and return the pan to the burner over medium-high heat. Add the mushrooms and sauté, stirring frequently, until they are nicely browned, 2 to 3 minutes per side. Remove and set aside with the bacon.
3. Pour off all but about 1 tablespoon of the remaining bacon fat. Return the pan to the burner, still over medium-high heat, add the onion, and sauté, stirring occasionally, until transparent, 5 to 7 minutes. Add the garlic and continue to sauté, stirring, 1 minute more. Add the sherry and red wine vinegar, and cook, stirring occasionally, for another minute. Remove the pan from the heat, add the oil, sugar, and salt and pepper, and mix well.
4. Place the spinach in a large bowl, add the warm dressing, and toss to coat. Add the reserved bacon and mushrooms, toss again, and serve at once.

Bibb Lettuce with Grilled Scallops, Sausage, and Pineapple

WITH MANGO-BLACK PEPPER DRESSING

I can't explain it, but when I think of scallops, I also think of sausage. Here I quickly blanch the scallops before grilling so that they firm up a bit and don't stick to the grill. Be sure to keep a close eye on them, though, because while they are as easy to grill as hot dogs, they do get tough if overcooked. This dressing, which pairs black pepper with the musky, mellow, aromatic flavor of the world's greatest fruit, the mango, is also excellent as a dressing for rice salad.

S E R V E S   4   T O   6

Best substitute greens: Boston lettuce or any other from Column A, page 18.

For the dressing

1	mango, peeled, pitted, and roughly chopped
⅓	cup red wine vinegar
½	cup olive oil
1	teaspoon minced garlic
3	tablespoons freshly cracked black pepper
¼	cup roughly chopped fresh cilantro
	Salt to taste

For the salad

2	round slices fresh pineapple, each about 1 inch thick, peeled
2	tablespoons molasses
2	pieces sausage of your choice, each about 4 ounces
½	pound sea scallops, blanched in boiling salted water for 1 minute, plunged into cold water to stop cooking, and drained
1	tablespoon olive oil
	Salt and freshly cracked black pepper to taste

    1   large head Bibb lettuce, any tough outer
        leaves removed, inner leaves washed, dried,
        and torn in half
    1   red bell pepper, seeded and diced large

1. Prepare a medium-hot fire in your grill.

2. Place the mango and vinegar in a blender or food processor and puree. With the motor still running, add the oil slowly. Turn off the motor, add the garlic, pepper, and cilantro, pulse to blend, and add salt. Set aside.

3. Grill the pineapple rounds over a medium-hot fire until they are seared and rather tender, 2 to 3 minutes per side. During the last minute of cooking, brush the pineapple with the molasses. Remove from the grill and cut each round into 8 pieces. Set aside.

4. Grill the sausages over a medium fire until cooked through, 5 to 6 minutes per side. Cut a thin slice from one piece and check to be sure the sausage is cooked all the way through. Remove from the grill, cut into thin rounds, and set aside with the pineapple.

5. Dry the scallops, sprinkle them with salt and pepper, and thread them onto skewers. Grill over a medium fire until just browned, 2 to 3 minutes per side. Remove from the grill and slide off the skewers into the bowl with the sausage and pineapple.

6. Place the lettuce and bell pepper in a large bowl. Add the pineapple, sausage, and scallops. Stir the dressing well, add just enough to moisten the ingredients (there will be some dressing left over), and toss to coat. Serve at once.

Mesclun with Grilled Foie Gras, Pears, and Maui Onion

WITH PORT WINE DRESSING

Don't give me that funny look—there is actually a long tradition of grilling foie gras in Israel. The high heat of grilling cooks the foie gras quickly, maintaining its inner tenderness while providing a flavorful sear on the outside. Since it is an expensive indulgence, though, keep a particularly close eye on it when it's over the fire; after it comes off, then turn your attention to the pears, and finally the onion. I would also use this dressing as a dipping sauce for quail or any other type of game bird.

S E R V E S   4   T O   6

Best substitute greens: Any baby greens or any from Column A, page 18.

For the dressing

- 1 cup port wine
- ½ small red onion, diced fine
- ½ cup orange juice (about 1 large orange)
- ⅓ cup olive oil
- 3 tablespoons balsamic vinegar

  Salt and freshly cracked black pepper to taste

For the salad

- 2 pears of your choice, halved and cored
- 1 large Maui onion, peeled and cut into slices about 1 inch thick (or substitute Walla Walla, Vidalia, or any other sweet onion)
- ¼ cup olive oil

  Salt and freshly cracked black pepper to taste
- 4 medallions of foie gras, 2 ounces each, ½ to ¾-inch thick (or substitute chicken livers)

  About 10 ounces mesclun
  (or substitute any other mixture of baby greens)

1. Prepare a medium-hot fire in your grill.

2. In a small saucepan, combine the port, red onion, and orange juice. Bring to a boil over high heat, reduce heat slightly, and boil until liquid is reduced to about ⅓ cup, 15 to 20 minutes. Remove from the heat, cool to room temperature, and whisk in the olive oil and vinegar. Season with salt and pepper and set aside.

3. Rub the pear halves and onion rings with oil and sprinkle them with salt and pepper. Sprinkle the foie gras with salt and pepper. Place the pears, onion, and foie gras on the grill over a medium-hot fire and grill until the foie gras is medium-rare (2 to 3 minutes per side), the onion is golden (3 to 4 minutes per side), and the pears are well browned (4 to 5 minutes per side). As soon as the pears are cool enough to handle, cut them into half-inch cubes.

4. Place the mesclun greens in a large bowl. Add the onion rings and pear chunks. Stir the dressing well, pour in just enough to moisten the ingredients (there will be some dressing left over), and toss to coat. Place on serving plates, top with foie gras, and serve at once.

Bitter Greens with Fried Oysters, Corn, and Pickled Onion

WITH TARTAR VINAIGRETTE

I've always been fond of fried oysters served with tartar sauce, so in this salad the vinaigrette is basically a kind of thin tartar sauce. The pickled onions are an easy, colorful, and tasty foil for the mellow oysters, but you can also leave them out if you haven't planned ahead enough to let them sit and pickle. The vinaigrette is also good for tuna or chicken salad.

S E R V E S   4   T O   6

Best substitute greens: Any from Columns B-1 or B-2, page 18.

For the dressing

- ½ cup mayonnaise, yours or mine (page 41)
- ¼ cup apple cider vinegar
- 2 tablespoons pickle relish
- 2 tablespoons Dijon mustard
- 2 tablespoons chopped fresh parsley
- 2 tablespoons capers (optional)
  Salt and freshly cracked black pepper to taste

For the salad

- 1 medium red onion, peeled, halved, and halves very thinly sliced
- ½ cup red wine vinegar
- 1 teaspoon grenadine (optional)
- 1 cup yellow cornmeal
- ½ teaspoon salt
- 1 teaspoon freshly cracked black pepper
  About 4 cups vegetable oil for deep-frying
- 1 pint freshly shucked oysters
  About 8 cups bitter greens (chicory, dandelion greens, escarole, baby mustard, arugula)

2   ears corn, blanched in boiling salted water for
2 minutes, drained, and kernels cut off the cob
(about 1 cup kernels)

1. In a medium bowl, combine the mayonnaise and vinegar, and whisk to blend. Add the pickle relish, mustard, parsley, and capers if you want them and mix well. Season with salt and pepper and set aside.

2. Place the onion slices in a small bowl and pour the vinegar and grenadine (if you have it) over the top. The onion should be completely covered by the liquid. Cover and refrigerate overnight or for at least 6 hours, stirring a couple of times.

3. In a small, flat bowl, combine the cornmeal, salt, and pepper and mix well. Pour enough oil into a medium saucepan to come to a depth of about 1 inch and heat over medium-high heat to approximately 350°F. (If you do not have a deep-frying thermometer, drop a small piece of bread in the oil; if the oil is the right temperature, the bread should sink to the bottom then immediately rise to the top and start bubbling.) Dredge the oysters in the cornmeal mixture, drop them into the hot oil a few at a time, and fry until golden brown, 1½ to 2 minutes. Remove and place on paper towels to drain. Repeat until all oysters have been fried.

4. Place the greens in a large bowl. Stir the dressing well, add just enough to moisten the greens (there will be some dressing left over), and toss to coat. Place the dressed greens on individual serving plates, top with the oysters and onion, and sprinkle with the corn kernels. Serve while the oysters are still warm.

Romaine with Buttermilk Fried Chicken Livers

WITH COTTAGE CHEESE DRESSING

The boys at the Blue Room—day chef Mark Romano and his associate Enrique Hernandez—are always frying up chicken livers during the day to snack on; here we combine them with lettuce, apples, and bacon in a rich salad. If you want to make this salad a little lighter, just omit the bacon.

SERVES 4 TO 6

Best substitute greens: Any from Column A, page 18.

For the dressing

- ½ cup cottage cheese
- 4 tablespoons apple cider vinegar
- 1 tablespoon sugar
- 1 tablespoon paprika
- ¼ cup thinly sliced white part of scallion
- Salt and freshly cracked black pepper to taste

For the salad

- 1 pound chicken livers
- 1 cup buttermilk
- 6 tablespoons vegetable oil
- 2 Granny Smith or other tart apples, cored and cut lengthwise into eighths
- 6 slices bacon
- 1 cup yellow cornmeal
- ½ cup all-purpose flour
- 1 teaspoon salt
- ½ teaspoon freshly cracked black pepper
- 1 head romaine lettuce, tough outer leaves removed, inner leaves washed, dried, and torn into halves or thirds
- 4 stalks celery, including leaves, diced large

1. In a medium bowl, combine all the dressing ingredients and stir well to combine. Set aside.

2. Place the chicken livers and buttermilk in a small, shallow bowl, making sure that the livers are completely covered by the milk. Allow to stand, covered and refrigerated, for at least 4 but no more than 24 hours.

3. In a large sauté pan, heat 2 tablespoons of the vegetable oil over medium-high heat until hot but not smoking. Add the apple slices and sauté, stirring as necessary to prevent sticking, until nicely browned, 1 to 2 minutes per side. Remove and set aside.

4. Sauté the bacon slices over medium heat until crisp, 6 to 8 minutes, then remove and drain on paper towels.

5. Drain the chicken livers and discard the buttermilk. In a small bowl, combine the cornmeal, flour, salt, and pepper and mix well. Dredge the livers in this mixture, shaking off any excess. Add the remaining 4 tablespoons of vegetable oil to the sauté pan and heat over medium-high heat until hot but not smoking. Add the chicken livers in small batches, being careful not to crowd them, and sauté until they are just crisp on the outside, 2 to 4 minutes per side. As the livers are cooked, remove and drain on paper towels. Repeat until all livers have been cooked.

6. In a large bowl, combine the romaine, celery, and apples. Stir the dressing well, add just enough to moisten the ingredients (there will be some dressing left over), and toss to coat. Place the dressed salad on individual serving plates, top with the hot chicken livers, crumble the bacon over the top, and serve at once.

Romaine Salad with Gorgonzola, Roasted Red Peppers, and Polenta Croutons

WITH SWEET BALSAMIC DRESSING

What my grandma always called cornmeal mush has recently become quite fashionable in its Italian incarnation as polenta. So here we make it into croutons and match it with strong-flavored Gorgonzola cheese and smoky roasted peppers in an Italian-inspired salad. To restore the grandma quotient a bit, we add some pickle relish to the dressing. This dressing also goes well spooned over grilled bread or serve with grilled chicken wings.

S E R V E S   4   T O   6

Best substitute greens: Arugula, dandelion greens, or any from Column A, page 18.

For the dressing

- ¾ cup olive oil
- ¼ cup balsamic vinegar
- 1 teaspoon minced garlic
- 1 tablespoon sugar
- 1 tablespoon dry mustard
- 1 tablespoon pickle relish
   Salt and freshly cracked black pepper to taste

For the salad

- 3 cups water
- 1 teaspoon salt
- 1½ cups yellow cornmeal
- ¼ cup grated Parmesan cheese
- ¼ cup chopped fresh basil (or substitute parsley)
   Salt and freshly cracked black pepper to taste
- ¼ cup olive oil

1   head romaine, tough outer leaves removed and
     inner leaves washed and dried

½ pound Gorgonzola cheese, diced large

2   roasted red bell peppers (page 42), cut
     into thin strips

1. In a small bowl, whisk together all the dressing ingredients until well blended. Set aside.

2. In a small saucepan, bring the water and salt to a boil over high heat. Reduce the heat to medium and add the cornmeal in a slow, steady stream, whisking constantly. Reduce heat to low and cook slowly for 20 to 30 minutes, stirring every 3 to 5 minutes, until the mixture is smooth and pulls away from the sides of the pan. Remove from heat, stir in the Parmesan and basil, season with salt and pepper, and pour onto a lightly greased shallow baking pan. Smooth out to an even thickness of about ¾ inch and cool in the refrigerator for about 1 hour. Remove from the refrigerator and cut into bite-size pieces.

3. In a large sauté pan, heat the olive oil over medium heat until hot but not smoking. Add the polenta cubes and fry until golden brown, 2 to 3 minutes. Remove to paper towels to drain.

4. Tear the romaine leaves in halves or thirds. In a large bowl, combine the romaine, Gorgonzola, and bell peppers. Stir the dressing well, pour on just enough to moisten the ingredients (there will be some dressing left over), and toss to coat. Place on individual serving plates, top with the warm croutons, and serve at once.

Baby Turnip Greens with Grilled Sweetbreads and Maui Onion

WITH DRIED APRICOT DRESSING

The mellow flavor and meltingly smooth texture of sweetbreads are made even more pleasing when enhanced by the slight smoky sear of grilling. Here they are combined with sweet onion—my favorite is Maui, but you can use any variety, even red onion in a pinch—and tender young turnip greens, which not only taste great but are reputed to be a good hangover cure. This dressing is also excellent on pork or lamb.

S E R V E S   4   T O   6

Best substitute greens: Young spinach or any baby cooking greens such as mustard, kale, beet, or chard.

For the dressing

- ¾ cup olive oil
- ¼ cup balsamic vinegar
- ¼ cup minced dried apricots
- ¼ cup chopped fresh parsley
- 1 tablespoon minced garlic
- 1 tablespoon grainy mustard
- 1 tablespoon sugar
  Salt and freshly cracked black pepper to taste

For the salad

- 1 pound veal sweetbreads
- ¼ cup white vinegar
- 1 teaspoon salt
- ½ teaspoon freshly cracked black pepper
- 1 large Maui or other sweet onion such as Vidalia, Walla Walla, or Texas Sweet, peeled and cut into 1-inch rings

2   tablespoons olive oil
    Salt and freshly cracked black pepper to taste
1   pound turnip greens, trimmed, washed, and dried

1. Prepare a medium-hot fire in your grill.

2. In a medium bowl, combine all the dressing ingredients and whisk together well. Set aside.

3. Place the sweetbreads, vinegar, salt, and pepper in a medium saucepan. Add enough cold water to cover the sweetbreads and bring to a simmer over high heat. Reduce the heat to medium and simmer until the sweetbreads are firm, 12 to 15 minutes. (The sweetbreads should feel like the base of your thumb when you press against it with your finger.) Remove from heat, drain, and allow to cool. As soon as they are cool enough to handle, separate the sweetbreads into bite-size nuggets and thread them onto skewers.

4. Rub the onion rings with oil and sprinkle with salt and pepper. Put the onion rings and the sweetbread skewers on the grill over a medium-hot fire and grill until onions and sweetbreads are both golden brown, 3 to 4 minutes per side for both. Remove from the grill and set aside.

5. Place the turnip greens in a large bowl. Stir the dressing well, add just enough to moisten the greens (there will be some dressing left over), and toss to coat. Place on a platter or individual serving plates, top with the onion rings and skewered sweetbreads, and serve at once.

Watercress with Green Grapes, Smoked Salmon, and Hard-Cooked Egg

WITH DILL-HORSERADISH DRESSING

Green grapes are wonderful in salads, providing sweetness, juiciness, and texture. In this salad, be particularly careful not to use too much dressing. If the watercress, grapes, and celery are just lightly coated, the rather intense flavors of the dressing make a nice counterpoint to the subtle, smoky taste of the salmon; but if you pour on too much, the fish becomes overpowered. If you have dressing left over, try mixing a bit into egg salad or spooning it over any cold fish.

S E R V E S   4   T O   6

Best substitute greens: Any from Column B-1 or B-2, page 18.

For the dressing

- ¾ cup olive oil
- ¼ cup sherry vinegar (or substitute red wine vinegar)
- ¼ cup roughly chopped fresh dill
- 2 tablespoons prepared horseradish
- 2 tablespoons capers
- 2 tablespoons grainy mustard
   Salt and freshly cracked black pepper to taste

For the salad

- 2 small bunches watercress, trimmed, washed, and dried
- ½ cup seedless green grapes, halved
- ½ cup celery, diced medium
- ¾ pound smoked salmon, sliced thin
- 2 hard-cooked eggs, chopped fine

1. In a medium bowl, combine all the dressing ingredients and whisk together well.

2. In a large bowl, combine the watercress and grapes. Stir the dressing well, add just enough to moisten the ingredients (there will be some dressing left over), and toss to coat. Place the dressed watercress and grapes on individual serving plates, top each with some of the sliced salmon, sprinkle with the chopped egg, and serve at once.

10

SALADS FOR
A CROWD

FEEDING A CROWD CAN BE A CHORE, or it can be one of life's great pleasures, in which food and drink provide a way to celebrate the joy of each other's company.

As everybody knows, the key to making your gatherings the fun kind rather than the uptight kind is for you to kick back and enjoy the meal along with your guests. The salads in this chapter are designed to help you do just that. With these recipes in hand, you can serve some drinks; set out some marinated olives, spiced nuts, or whatever other snacks you have around the house; and toss together a salad that will satisfy the whole crowd.

Many of these recipes include grilled ingredients, which gives you the chance to stand around and cook while shooting the breeze with your guests, then combine the ingredients and serve them while they're still warm from the grill. If you want, you can use one of the dressings, like the Spicy Sesame-Lime Dressing, to coat some chicken wings that you grill up for folks to munch on while you cook.

On the other hand, if you're one of those folks who truly relaxes only when everything is ready, choose a salad like Baby Asian Greens with Ginger-Rubbed Chicken and Apricots, so you can prepare each component of the salad before the company arrives, then toss the components together at the last minute. Whatever makes you feel most like hanging around with your friends is the way to go.

Sweet and Sour Cabbage Salad with Summer Vegetables

WITH ICE CUBE VINAIGRETTE

When I was a child, I noticed that my mother often put ice cubes in her vinegar dressing. I thought it was weird at the time, but when I later tried it myself I found that the ice cubes serve two purposes: they dilute the vinegar, and the resulting very cold dressing keeps the cabbage and cucumbers crisp. All in all, it makes a great salad for a hot August day.

SERVES 8 TO 10

Best substitute greens: Any from Column D, page 19.

For the dressing

- ½ cup olive oil
- 2 cups apple cider vinegar
- ½ cup sugar
- ¼ cup celery seeds
  Salt and freshly cracked black pepper to taste
- 6 ice cubes

For the salad

- 1 small head red cabbage, outer leaves removed, remaining leaves cut into very thin slices
- 1 small head green cabbage, outer leaves removed, remaining leaves cut into very thin slices
- 2 cups loosely packed fresh parsley leaves
- 4 ears corn, blanched in boiling salted water for 2 minutes, drained, and kernels cut off the cob (about 2 cups kernels)
- 2 cucumbers, peeled if you want to, cut into ½-inch rounds
- 1 large red onion, peeled, halved, and thinly sliced

continued

1. In a medium bowl, combine all the dressing ingredients except the ice cubes and whisk together well. Add the ice cubes, stir for a minute or two, and set aside.

2. In a large bowl, combine all the salad ingredients. Add all of the dressing, toss to coat, and serve immediately.

Arugula with Grilled Prosciutto and Figs

WITH CHUNKY ROASTED PEPPER VINAIGRETTE

Fresh figs, prosciutto, and hard cheese are a classic Italian combination. Here we grill the figs and prosciutto to add a little smoky flavor, then combine them with arugula, a green that originated in Italy. If you can't get your hands on prosciutto, you can use any country ham—Smithfield is my personal choice—sliced very thin and grilled. Get some crusty peasant-style bread and a bottle of red wine, and this salad makes an awesome meal. Toss leftover dressing with pasta or dunk bread into it.

S E R V E S   8   T O   1 0

Best substitute greens: Any from Column B-2, page 18.

For the dressing

- 1½ cups olive oil
- ¼ cup red wine vinegar
- ¼ cup balsamic vinegar
- 2 tablespoons minced garlic
- 4 roasted red peppers (page 43), cleaned and diced small
- 1 cup roughly chopped fresh basil

Salt and freshly cracked black pepper to taste

For the salad

10 fresh figs, halved

2   tablespoons vegetable oil

Salt and freshly cracked black pepper to taste

1   pound prosciutto, thinly sliced

5   bunches arugula, trimmed, washed, and dried

1   pound provolone, cut into small wedges or slices (optional)

1. Prepare a medium-hot fire in your grill.

2. In a small bowl, combine all the dressing ingredients and mix very well. Set aside.

3. Rub the figs with the oil, sprinkle with salt and pepper, and grill over a medium-hot fire, cut side down, until nicely browned, 3 to 4 minutes. At the same time, grill the prosciutto slices for about 1 minute on one side only, just long enough to brown them a bit.

4. Place the arugula in a large bowl. Stir the dressing well, add just enough to moisten the arugula (you will have some dressing left over), and toss well. Place on a serving platter, top with the figs, prosciutto, and provolone, if using, and serve.

Arugula and Radicchio with Grilled Mozzarella and Bread Skewers

WITH BASIL-PINE NUT DRESSING

The Mediterranean flavors of this salad make it an excellent choice for vegetarians who want food that is deeply flavorful but still familiar. Be sure that you grill the skewers over a medium rather than a hot fire, or you risk melting the cheese into the coals. To check the fire temperature, hold your hand about 5 inches from the grill surface; if you can hold it there for 4 to 5 seconds, you have a medium fire. This dressing is fantastic with cold lamb or as a dressing for a simple white bean salad.

SERVES 8 TO 10

Best substitute greens: Any from Columns B-1or B-2, page 18.

For the dressing

¼ cup pine nuts, toasted in a 350°F. oven for 7 to 10 minutes until golden

4 cloves garlic, peeled

1 cup loosely packed fresh basil leaves

¼ cup grainy mustard

1½ cups olive oil

¼ cup red wine vinegar

¼ cup fresh lemon juice (about 1 large lemon)
Salt and freshly cracked black pepper to taste

For the salad

1 pound fresh mozzarella, diced large (about 16 pieces)

16 1-inch squares good-quality day-old baguette or peasant bread
Salt and freshly cracked black pepper to taste

3 bunches arugula, trimmed, washed, and dried

2 heads radicchio, outer leaves discarded, inner leaves cored and sliced very thin

3   medium tomatoes, cored and quartered
½   cup Kalamata or other briny black olives (optional)

1. Prepare a medium fire in your grill.

2. Combine the pine nuts, garlic, basil, and mustard in a blender or food processor and puree. With the motor still running, add the oil in a steady stream. Turn off the motor, add the vinegar and lemon juice and pulse to blend. Season with salt and pepper. Set aside.

3. Thread the mozzarella and bread cubes alternately onto skewers and sprinkle them with salt and pepper. Grill over a medium fire until the bread is nicely browned and the cheese begins to melt, 2 to 3 minutes per side.

4. In a large bowl, combine the arugula, radicchio, tomatoes, and olives, if you want them. Stir the dressing well, add just enough to moisten the ingredients (you will have some dressing left over), and toss to coat. Slide the mozzarella and bread cubes off the skewers onto the top of the salad and serve.

Baby Asian Greens with Ginger-Rubbed Chicken and Apricots

WITH GINGERY LEMONGRASS DRESSING

This one is for folks who like intense flavors in their food. It's best when made with a mixture of the bitter baby Asian greens now available in the United States—mizuna, tatsoi, baby mustard greens, komatsu, baby bok choy, pea shoots, even baby chrysanthemum leaves—but if you can't get your hands on a variety of these greens, any one or two will do the trick. To add to the flavor intensity, we follow the Asian practice of using whole herb leaves as greens, going with the distinctly Southeast Asian trio of mint, coriander, and basil. The dressing also makes a fine dip for grilled chicken wings or shrimp, or a marinade for sliced raw cucumbers and carrots.

SERVES 8 TO 10

Best substitute greens: Mixture of any from Columns B-2 or C, pages 18–19.

For the dressing

5	stalks lemongrass, roughly chopped
3	tablespoons minced fresh ginger
1	cup white vinegar
1	cup water
¼	cup sugar
¼	cup sesame oil
½	cup vegetable oil
¼	cup soy sauce
¼	cup fish sauce (optional)

For the salad

½	cup roughly chopped fresh cilantro
¼	cup minced fresh ginger
¼	cup cracked coriander seeds
¼	cup cracked white pepper (or substitute black pepper)

2   tablespoons crushed star anise
    (or substitute 1 tablespoon five-spice powder)

⅓   cup vegetable oil

2   tablespoons salt

3   pounds boneless chicken breast
    (about 8 single breasts)
    About 1½ pounds mixed baby Asian greens

2   red bell peppers, seeded and diced large

6   apricots, pitted and quartered

1   cup whole fresh cilantro leaves

¼   cup whole fresh mint leaves

¼   cup whole fresh basil leaves

1. In a medium saucepan, combine the lemongrass, ginger, vinegar, water, and sugar and bring to a boil over high heat. Reduce the heat to low and simmer for 1 hour. Remove from heat and strain, discarding solids; you should have about 1 cup liquid. Add the sesame oil, vegetable oil, soy sauce, and fish sauce, if you want, and mix well. Set aside.

2. Prepare a medium-hot fire in your grill.

3. In a small bowl, combine the chopped cilantro, ginger, coriander, pepper, star anise, vegetable oil, and salt and mix well. Rub the chicken breasts thoroughly with this mixture, then grill them over a medium-hot fire until they are opaque throughout, 3 to 4 minutes on the first side and 2 to 3 minutes on the other. Check for doneness by cutting into the thickest breast to see if it is opaque all the way through. Remove the breasts from the grill and set them aside to cool.

continued

4. In a large bowl, combine the Asian greens, bell peppers, apricots, and herb leaves. Cut each of the chicken breasts into 5 or 6 slices and add to the bowl. Stir the dressing well, pour on just enough to moisten the ingredients (you will have some dressing left over), toss gently to coat, and serve.

Tommy's Red Cabbage Salad with Grilled Pineapple

WITH SPICY SESAME-LIME DRESSING

My nephew Tommy is a budding master of the grill, and like most kids he loves to push the envelope, which he sometimes does by grilling fruit. Pineapple is one of his favorites, and he has mastered getting just the right glaze. Since he also likes red cabbage and Asian flavors, this salad is right up his alley. This dressing is also outstanding over grilled chicken wings or as a barbecue sauce with pork.

SERVES 8 TO 10

Best substitute greens: Any from Column D, page 19.

For the dressing

½ cup fresh orange juice (about 1 large orange)

¼ cup fresh lime juice (about 2 medium limes)

¼ cup sesame oil

6 tablespoons rice wine vinegar
(or substitute white vinegar)

¼ cup molasses

2 tablespoons minced fresh ginger

9 dashes Tabasco sauce

2 tablespoons crushed star anise
(or substitute 1 tablespoon five-spice powder)

¼ cup roughly chopped fresh cilantro
Salt and freshly cracked black pepper to taste

For the salad

  ¼ cup butter

  ¼ cup light or dark brown sugar

  1 medium pineapple, peeled and sliced into rounds
     about 1 inch thick (about 8 rounds)

  1 medium head red cabbage, cored and
     cut into thin strips

  1½ cups shredded carrots (about 2 medium carrots)

  1 bunch scallions, trimmed and thinly sliced
     (white and green parts)

1. Prepare a medium-hot fire in your grill.

2. In a small bowl, combine all the dressing ingredients and mix well. Set aside.

3. In a small saucepan, melt the butter over very low heat. Add the brown sugar, stir well to combine, and remove from heat.

4. Grill the pineapple rounds over a medium-hot fire until nicely browned, 2 to 3 minutes per side. During the last minute of cooking, brush the top sides liberally with the butter-sugar glaze. Remove from the grill and cut each round into eighths.

5. In a large bowl, combine the pineapple with the cabbage, carrots, and scallions. Stir the dressing well, add just enough to moisten the ingredients (you will have some dressing left over), toss well, and serve.

Romaine and Grilled Eggplant with Feta and Green Grapes

WITH CHUNKY CUCUMBER-TOMATO DRESSING

Eggplant has an outstanding tradition as a grilled vegetable. If you slap it on the grill right after you cut it up, in my opinion it doesn't have to be salted and drained to remove the bitterness, and without this process it has a better texture. In this Middle Eastern–inspired salad, the sweet juiciness of the grapes is a nice contrast to the creamy eggplant and the sharp feta cheese. This dressing is also good with grilled fish or as a kind of relish served with roast chicken.

S E R V E S   8   T O   1 0

Best substitute greens: Any from Column A, page 18.

For the dressing

1½	cups olive oil
½	cup red wine vinegar
2	tablespoons minced garlic
1	medium tomato, cored and diced small
1	cucumber, peeled, seeded, and diced small
½	cup pitted and roughly chopped Kalamata or other briny black olives
¼	cup chopped fresh oregano (or substitute basil or parsley)
2	tablespoons cumin seeds, toasted in a sauté pan over medium heat, shaken frequently, until fragrant, 2 to 3 minutes (or substitute 1 tablespoon ground cumin) Salt and freshly cracked black pepper to taste

For the salad

2	large eggplants, cut into ½-inch circles
¼	cup olive oil
	Salt and freshly cracked black pepper to taste

2 large heads romaine, tough outer leaves removed,
inner leaves washed, dried, and torn in halves or
thirds

½ pound feta cheese, crumbled (about 1 cup)

1 cup green seedless grapes, halved

1. Prepare a medium-hot fire in your grill.

2. In a medium bowl, combine the olive oil and vinegar and
whisk to combine. Add all the remaining dressing ingredients and
stir well to mix. Set aside.

3. Rub the eggplant circles with the olive oil, sprinkle with salt
and pepper, and grill over a medium-hot fire until well browned
and cooked through, 3 to 4 minutes per side. Remove from the
grill and, as soon as they are cool enough to handle, cut into
quarters and place in a large bowl.

4. Add the romaine, feta cheese, and grapes. Stir the dressing
well, add just enough to moisten the ingredients (you will have
some dressing left over), toss well, and serve.

Tomato and Bread Salad
WITH LEMON-PARSLEY DRESSING

The dressing for this salad, a variation on the bread salads of Italy and the Middle East, is more acidic than most dressings because the high proportion of vinegar and lemon juice softens the bread perfectly. The dressing is also very garlicky, so if you're not a garlic lover you might want to ease up on that ingredient a bit. Be sure you make the bread cubes large enough so that when you toast them they get crisp on the outside but stay soft on the inside. If you like roasted root vegetables, try dipping them in this dressing.

S E R V E S   8   T O   1 0

Best substitute greens: Any from Column B-2, page 18.

For the dressing

½   cup extra-virgin olive oil

¼   cup fresh lemon juice (about 1 large lemon)

½   cup red wine vinegar

2   tablespoons minced garlic

½   cup roughly chopped fresh parsley leaves

Salt and freshly cracked black pepper to taste

For the salad

3   cucumbers, peeled if you want to, diced medium

3   large tomatoes, cored and diced medium

1   large red onion, peeled and diced medium

½   cup pitted Kalamata or other briny black olives

5   cups 1-inch bread cubes, toasted in a 350°F. oven until browned, 10 to 15 minutes

3   bunches arugula, trimmed, washed, and dried

1   pound good-quality Parmesan cheese

1. In a medium bowl, combine all the dressing ingredients and whisk together.

2. Place all salad ingredients except the Parmesan cheese in a large bowl. Add enough dressing just to moisten the ingredients (you will have some dressing left over), toss well, and place on a large platter.

3. Using a cheese shaver or vegetable peeler, shave the Parmesan cheese over the top of the salad and serve.

Arugula with Grilled Vegetables and Fresh Mozzarella

WITH LEMON-HERB DRESSING

Tom Huth, the architect who designed the Blue Room and East Coast Grill, is well known around Boston for "Salad Huth," which he brings to every dinner party. This is a variation of that salad, in which we grill the vegetables to add a little smoky flavor to the mix. It's is a fantastic way to use up that bumper crop of summer vegetables from your garden. If you haven't got any arugula, substitute a couple of small heads of romaine lettuce. Pass the dressing separately so people can use it on the vegetables or just on the arugula, as they please.

S E R V E S   8   T O   1 0

Best substitute greens: Any from Column B-1, page 18.

For the dressing

- 1½ cups olive oil
- ¼ cup fresh lemon juice (about 1 large lemon)
- ¼ cup balsamic vinegar
- Cloves from 2 heads roasted garlic (page 42), cleaned
- ¼ cup fresh herbs (parsley, sage, rosemary, thyme, or oregano, alone or in combination)
- 4 dashes Tabasco sauce
- Salt and freshly cracked black pepper to taste

For the salad

- 2 red bell peppers, seeded and halved lengthwise
- 3 plum tomatoes, halved lengthwise
- 2 medium red onions, peeled and cut into rings ½-inch thick
- 1 small eggplant, cut into rounds ½-inch thick
- 10 button mushrooms, stems trimmed

10 small Red Bliss potatoes, cooked in boiling salted
   water until easily pierced with a fork, 20 to 30
   minutes, then drained and halved
⅓ cup olive oil
   Salt and freshly cracked black pepper to taste
3 bunches arugula, trimmed, washed, and dried
1 pound fresh mozzarella, thinly sliced (optional)
1 cup pitted Kalamata or other briny black olives
   (optional)

1. Prepare a medium-hot fire in your grill.

2. In a medium bowl, combine all the dressing ingredients and whisk together well. Set aside.

3. Put the peppers, tomatoes, onions, eggplant, mushrooms, and potatoes in a very large bowl. Add the olive oil and salt and pepper, and toss well to coat the vegetables with oil. Grill the vegetables over a medium-hot fire until well browned, 4 to 6 minutes per side. Remove from the grill, and as soon as cool enough to handle, cut into smaller, bite-size pieces.

4. Make a bed of arugula on a large, shallow platter. Arrange the grilled vegetables on top of the arugula, top with the mozzarella and olives if you want, and pass dressing separately.

Index

Any of the salads in *Lettuce in Your Kitchen* may be served as a main course if the serving size is increased. However, certain recipes were specifically designed to serve as main courses and each is indicated by a bullet (•) following the page number on which it appears.

apples:
frisée with cucumbers, walnuts and, 124–125
green, romaine lettuce with stuffed tortillas and, 202–203
watercress and ham, salad of, 131–132
apricots:
baby Asian greens with ginger-rubbed chicken and, 246–248
and lamb skewers, grilled, spinach salad with, 182–183 •
artichokes, baby, red leaf lettuce with grilled figs and, 100–101
arugula, arugula salad, 17, 18, 27
bitter greens with fiery seared squid, 190–191
bitter greens with fried oysters, corn and pickled onions, 228–229
with black beans, corn and avocado, 108–109
in chef's salad with ribs, 142–143
with dried tomatoes, grilled red onions and Parmesan, 64–65
and duck salad with mango, caramelized onions and spiced pecans, 188–189 •
with fried green tomatoes, 112–113
grapefruit and orange salad, 62–63
with grilled fennel and fried garlic, 110–111
grilled lamb and lima beans, salad of, 134–135 •
with grilled prosciutto and figs, 242–243
with grilled vegetables and fresh mozzarella, 254–255
with lobster and pancetta, 217
local salad Johnson, 50–51
with pepper-crusted quail and pumpernickel croutons, 164–165 •
and radicchio with grilled mozzarella and bread skewers, 244–245
with red snapper ceviche and papaya, 132–133

with sautéed softshell crabs and toast points, 162–163 •
and seared sirloin salad, 218–219 •
and warm grill-roasted beet salad, 97–98
weight of, 23
with white beans and shrimp, 136–137
Asian greens, 17, 27–29
baby, with ginger-rubbed chicken and apricots, 246–248
asparagus:
hearts of romaine with roasted beets and, 106–107
oak leaf lettuce with grilled sweet potato and, 98–99
watercress with poached mussels and, 210–211
avocados:
arugula salad with black beans, corn and, 108–109
Bibb lettuce with poached shrimp, cornbread croutons and, 168–169 •
Boston lettuce, mango, and cucumber, salad of, 52–53
hearts of palm and cabbage salad with mangoes and, 196–197
romaine and tortilla salad with, 204–205
romaine lettuce, and tomato salad with cornbread croutons, 86–87
in romaine lettuce with green apples and stuffed tortillas, 202–203
in Southwestern Caesar salad, 60–61

bacon, 49
chicory salad with sweet potato and lemon-flavored crumbs, 146–147
Grandma Wetzler's escarole salad with eggs, potatoes and, 54–55
wilted spinach salad with shiitake mushrooms and, 222–223

basil, 19
  in baby Asian greens with ginger-rubbed
    chicken and apricots, 247
  in fancy greens with tomatoes and grilled
    garlic-herb bread, 84–85
  in leaf lettuce with grilled scallops, peppers
    and green olives, 174–175 •
  local salad Johnson, 50–51
  in spicy cabbage salad with chile-rubbed
    flank steak, 170–171 •
  and tomato salad, August, 81
beef:
  arugula and seared sirloin salad, 218–219
  spicy cabbage salad with chile-rubbed flank
    steak, 170–171 •
beet greens, salad of young cooking greens,
  49
beets:
  and arugula salad, warm grill-roasted, 97–
    98
  hearts of romaine with roasted asparagus and,
    106–107
  watercress and radicchio salad with leeks
    and, 122–123
Belgian endive, 18, 30
  watercress and radicchio with smoked
    salmon, 150–151
Bibb lettuce, 17, 18
  with grilled scallops, sausage and pineapple,
    224–225
  Iowa lettuce salad, 47
  with poached shrimp, avocado and
    cornbread croutons, 168–169 •
bitter greens:
  with fiery seared squid, 190–191
  with fried oysters, corn and pickled onion,
    228–229
black beans, 33
  arugula salad with corn, avocado and, 108–
    109
black-eyed peas, chicory with garlic pork,
    pickles and, 172–173 •
blue cheese:
  Boston lettuce with tomato and, 82
  green leaf lettuce with grilled peaches and,
    198–199
  watercress and endive salad with pears and,
    120–121
Boston lettuce, 17, 18
  crabmeat and mango, salad of, 187
  with grilled new potatoes and red onion
    rings, 74–75
  with grilled pork and pineapple, 192–193
  Iowa lettuce salad, 47
  local salad Johnson, 50–51
  mango, cucumber and avocado, salad of, 52–
    53
  in P.L.T. salad with giant black olive
    croutons, 92–93
  with poached salmon, peas and sweet potato,
    138–139
  with tomato and blue cheese, 82
  weight of, 23
bread:
  grilled garlic-herb, fancy greens with, 84–85

and mozzarella skewers, grilled, arugula and
  radicchio with, 244–245
and tomato salad, 252–253
bulgur, parsley and tomato salad with feta
  cheese and, 83

Cabbage, green, 17, 19
  and hearts of palm with avocados and
    mangoes, 196–197
  salad, Yucatán, 212–213
  salad with poached shrimp and hearts of
    palm, mixed, 140–141
  salad with summer vegetables, sweet and
    sour, 241–242
  weight of, 23
cabbage, red, 17, 19
  and hearts of palm with avocados and
    mangoes, 196–197
  salad with grilled pineapple, Tommy's, 248–249
  salad with poached shrimp and hearts of
    palm, 140–141
  salad with summer vegetables, sweet and
    sour, 241–242
  weight of, 23
cabbages, 17, 19, 23, 29
  see also napa cabbage
Caesar salad:
  with lots of garlic croutons, regulation, 58–59
  Southwestern, 60–61
cannellini, arugula salad with shrimp and, 136–
  137
ceviche, red snapper, arugula salad with
  papaya and, 132–133
chard, salad of young cooking greens, 49
chef's salad with ribs, 142–143
chicken:
  ginger-rubbed, baby Asian greens with
    apricots and, 246–248
  grilled, and watercress salad with mangoes
    and grapes, 159–160 •
  livers, buttermilk fried, with romaine, 230–231
  roast, spinach salad with peaches and, 180–
    181 •
chicory, 18, 30
  bitter greens with fiery seared squid, 190–191
  bitter greens with fried oysters, corn and
    pickled onions, 228–229
  with garlic pork, pickles and black-eyed peas,
    172–173 •
  and roasted pear salad, 66–67
  salad with sweet potato, bacon and lemon-
    flavored crumbs, 146–147
chile peppers, 33
Chinese cabbage, *see* napa cabbage
chipotle peppers, 34
chrysanthemum leaves, 28
cilantro, 19, 34
  in aromatic watercress, tomato and herb
    salad, 90–91
  in baby Asian greens with ginger-rubbed
    chicken and apricots, 247
  in romaine lettuce with green apples and
    stuffed tortillas, 202–203
  in spicy cabbage salad with chile-rubbed
    flank steak, 170–171 •

clams, mesclun with roasted pancetta and, 144–145
collard greens, in salad of young cooking greens, 49
cooking greens, young (baby), 29–30
    salad of, 49
coriander seeds, 34
corn:
    arugula salad with black beans, avocado and, 108–109
    bitter greens with fried oysters, pickled onion and, 228–229
cornbread:
    Bibb lettuce with croutons, poached shrimp, avocado and, 168–169 •
    croutons, romaine, tomato and avocado salad with, 86–87
    in Southwestern Caesar salad, 60–61
crabs, crabmeat:
    Boston lettuce and mango, salad of, 187
    softshell, sautéed, arugula with toast points and, 162–163 •
croutons:
    black olive, giant, P.L.T. salad with, 92–93
    garlic, regulation Caesar salad with lots of, 58–59
    goat cheese, baby greens with, 220–221
    polenta, romaine salad with Gorgonzola, roasted red peppers and, 232–233
    pumpernickel, arugula salad with pepper-crusted quail and, 164–165 •
cucumbers:
    Boston lettuce, mango and avocado, salad of, 52–53
    in escarole with papayas and fried plantains, 194–195
    frisée with apple and walnuts, 124–125
    leaf lettuce with tomato, feta and, 88–89
    local salad Johnson, 50–51
    in romaine with turnips and pomegranate seeds, 206–207
    in sweet and sour cabbage salad with summer vegetables, 241–242
cumin seeds, 34

daikon, 35
    salad of mizuna and #1 tuna with, 200–201
dandelion greens, 18, 30
    bitter greens with fiery seared squid, 190–191
    bitter greens with fried oysters, corn and pickled onions, 228–229
    with nectarines and Smithfield ham, 68–69
    weight of, 23
dressing, 20–21
    bacon-vinegar, 54–55
    basil-pine nut, 244–245
    black olive, 180–181
    charred tomato, 172–173
    charred tomato-lime, 168–169
    chile-beet, 116–117
    chunky avocado, 178–179
    chunky blue cheese, 66–67
    chunky cucumber-mint, 118–119
    chunky cucumber-tomato, 250–251

citrus-chipotle, 202–203
cottage cheese, 230–231
creamy balsamic, 64–65
creamy chile, 60–61
creamy horseradish, 131–132
creamy roasted garlic–Parmesan, 182–183
creamy roasted red pepper–orange, 100–101
creamy tarragon, 160–161
curry-chutney, 208–209
dill-horseradish, 236–237
dried apricot, 234–235
fau • Catalina, 198–199
ginger-soy, 154–155
gingery lemongrass, 246–248
Greek-style, 88–89
green herb, 132–133
green olive, 56–57
honey-sage, 152–153
lemon-caper, 218–219
lemon-herb, 254–255
lemon-lime, 187
lemon-parsley, 252–253
lime-peanut, 170–171
limey avocado, 140–141
mango–black pepper, 224–225
neo-green goddess, 138–139
orange-beet, 120–121
orange-chile, 108–109
orange–dill–sour cream, 98–99
orange-horseradish, 122–123
orange-saffron, 210–211
orange-spice, creamy, 52–53
peanut-molasses, 68–69
pickled ginger, 200–201
pineapple-chipotle, 212–213
port wine, 226–227
red pepper–orange, 100–101
roasted red pepper, 134–135
roast tomato-chile, 204–205
sesame, 166–167
simple cream, 47
smooth avocado, 217
spicy hoisin, 70–71
spicy sesame-lime, 248–249
sweet and spicy green peppercorn, 192–193
sweet balsamic, 232–233
sweet corn, 112–113
sweet red onion–cumin, 102–103
sweet-sour bacon, 164–165
sweet-sour French, 146–147
tamarind-lime, 194–195
tartar sauce, tidewater, 162–163
Thousand Island, 48, 106–107
tomato-corn salsa, 148–149
tomato-garlic, warm, 144–145
warm pancetta, 49
warm sherry, 222–223
yogurt-coriander, 206–207
yogurt-mint, 124–125
    see also vinaigrette
duck and arugula salad with mango, caramelized onions and spiced pecans, 188–189 •

eggplant:
grilled, and romaine with feta and green
grapes, 250–251
spinach salad with peppers, roasted garlic
and, 114–115
eggs:
Grandma Wetzler's escarole salad with
bacon, potatoes and, 54–55
hard-cooked, watercress with green grapes,
smoked salmon and, 236–237
in watercress, endive and radicchio with
smoked salmon, 150–151
endive, 17, 30
watercress and radicchio with smoked
salmon, 150–151
and watercress salad with pears and blue
cheese, 120–121
escarole, 17, 18, 30
bitter greens with fiery seared squid, 190–191
with papayas and fried plantains, 194–195
salad with bacon, eggs and potatoes,
Grandma Wetzler's, 54–55
weight of, 23

fennel, 35
Cary's leaf lettuce salad with orange, red
onion and, 56–57
grilled, arugula salad with fried garlic and,
110–111
feta cheese:
leaf lettuce with tomato, cucumber and, 88–89
parsley and tomato salad with bulgur and, 83
romaine and grilled eggplant with green
grapes and, 250–251
figs:
arugula with grilled prosciutto and, 242–243
red leaf lettuce with grilled baby artichokes
and, 100–101
fish sauce, 35
five-spice powder, 36
flank steak, chile-rubbed, spicy cabbage salad
with, 170–171 •
foie gras, pears and Maui onions, grilled,
mesclun with, 226–227
frisée, 18, 30
with apple, cucumber and walnuts, 124–125
bitter greens with fiery seared squid, 190–191
weight of, 23

garlic:
chips, Doctor Hibachi's spinach salad with
roasted peppers, grilled lamb with, 152–153 •
chips, red leaf lettuce with grapes, manchego
cheese and, 76–77
croutons, regulation Caesar salad with lots of,
58–59
fried, arugula salad with grilled fennel and,
110–111
-herb bread, grilled, with fancy greens,
84–85
pork, chicory with pickles, black-eyed peas
and, 172–173 •
roasted, 42

roasted, spinach salad with peppers, eggplant
and, 114–115
goat cheese:
croutons, baby greens with, 220–221
romaine salad with navy beans and, 104–
105
Gorgonzola, romaine salad with roasted red
peppers, polenta croutons and, 232–233
grapefruit, arugula and orange salad, 62–63
grapes, green:
romaine and grilled eggplant with feta and,
250–251
smoked salmon and hard-cooked egg,
watercress with, 236–237
watercress and grilled chicken salad with
mangoes and, 159–160 •
grapes, red leaf lettuce with manchego
cheese, garlic chips and, 76–77
green beans:
red leaf lettuce with peppered tuna, olives
and, 160–161 •
romaine lettuce with sausage, peppers and,
176–177 •
greens, 14–17
cleaning, 15
drying and storing, 15–16
fancy, with tomatoes and grilled garlic-herb
bread, 84–85
measurement of, 22–23
nutritional value of, 10–11
substitutions for, 16–17

ham:
Smithfield, dandelion greens with nectarines
and, 68–69
watercress and apple, salad of, 131–132
hearts of palm:
and cabbage salad with avocados and
mangoes, 196–197
mi•ed cabbage salad with poached shrimp
and, 140–141
hearts of romaine with roasted beets and
asparagus, 106–107
herbs:
-garlic bread, grilled, with fancy greens, 84–85
as greens, 19
in watercress and tomato salad, aromatic, 90–
91
hiziki, 36
hoisin sauce, 36

iceberg lettuce, 17, 19
your classic wedge of, 48
ingredients guide, 26–42
Iowa lettuce salad, 47

jalapeño pepper, 36
jicama, 36
red leaf lettuce with tangerines and, 102–103

kale, 17
salad of young cooking greens, 49
komatsu, 28
kosher salt, 37

lamb:
   and apricot skewers, grilled, spinach salad
      with, 182–183 •
   Doctor Hibachi's spinach salad with grilled
      roasted peppers and garlic chips and,
      152–153 •
   grilled, arugula and lima beans, salad of,
      134–135 •
leeks, watercress and radicchio salad with
   beets and, 122–123
lemon-flavored crumbs, chicory salad with
   bacon, sweet potato and, 146–147
lemongrass, 37
lentils, and spinach salad with toasted walnuts,
   116–117
lettuce, 18, 31
   of choice with grilled new potatoes and red
      onion rings, 74–75
   leaf, salad with orange, fennel and red onion,
      Cary's, 56–57
   salad, Iowa, 47
lettuce, green leaf, 17, 18
   with grilled new potatoes and red onion
      rings, 74–75
   with grilled peaches and blue cheese, 198–199
   with grilled scallops, peppers and green
      olives, 174–175 •
   with tomato, cucumber and feta, 88–89
   weight of, 23
lettuce, red leaf, 17, 18
   with grapes, manchego cheese and garlic
      chips, 76–77
   with grilled figs and baby artichokes, 100–
      101
   with grilled new potatoes and red onion
      rings, 74–75
   with grilled scallops, peppers and green
      olives, 174–175 •
   Iowa lettuce salad, 47
   with peppered tuna, green beans and olives,
      160–161 •
   with tangerines and jicama, 102–103
   weight of, 23
lima beans, arugula and grilled lamb, salad of,
   134–135 •
livers, chicken, buttermilk fried, romaine with,
   230–231
lobster, arugula with pancetta and, 217
local salad Johnson, 50–51

manchego cheese, red leaf lettuce with
   grapes, garlic chips and, 76–77
mangoes, 37
   arugula and duck salad with caramelized
      onions, spiced pecans and, 188–189 •
   Boston lettuce, cucumber and avocado, salad
      of, 52–53
   Boston lettuce and crabmeat, salad of,
      187
   hearts of palm and cabbage salad with
      avocados and, 196–197
   spinach salad with potato and, 208–209
   watercress and grilled chicken salad, grapes
      and, 159–160 •

Maui onions:
   foie gras and pears, grilled, mesclun with,
      226–227
   and sweetbreads, grilled, baby turnip greens
      with, 234–235
mayonnaise, homemade, 41
measurements, 22–23
mesclun, 31–32
   with grilled foie gras, pears and Maui onion,
      226–227
   with roasted clams and pancetta, 144–145
mint, 19
   in aromatic watercress, tomato and herb
      salad, 90–91
   in baby Asian greens with ginger-rubbed
      chicken and apricots, 247
   in spicy cabbage salad with chile-rubbed
      flank steak, 170–171 •
mizuna, 18, 28
   bitter greens with fiery seared squid, 190–
      191
   and #1 tuna with daikon, salad of, 200–201
mozzarella:
   arugula with grilled vegetables and fresh,
      254–255
   and bread skewers, grilled, arugula and
      radicchio with, 244–245
mushrooms, shiitake, wilted spinach salad with
   bacon and, 222–223
mussels, poached, watercress with asparagus
   and, 210–211
mustard greens:
   baby, 28
   baby, in bitter greens with fiery seared squid,
      190–191
   salad of young cooking greens, 49

napa cabbage, 17, 19, 28
   salad with chile-rubbed flank steak, spicy,
      170–171 •
   Southeast Asian–style slaw, 126–127
   weight of, 23
navy beans, romaine salad with goat cheese
   and, 104–105
nectarines, dandelion greens with Smithfield
   ham and, 68–69
new potatoes, lettuce of choice with grilled red
   onion rings and, 74–75
noodles, rice, and watercress salad with grilled
   quail, 166–167 •

oak leaf lettuce, 17, 18
   with grilled new potatoes and red onion
      rings, 74–75
   with grilled sweet potato and asparagus, 98–
      99
   Iowa lettuce salad, 47
   local salad Johnson, 50–51
olive oil, 35
olives:
   green, leaf lettuce with grilled scallops,
      peppers and, 174–175 •
   red leaf lettuce with peppered tuna, green
      beans and, 160–161 •

onions:
caramelized, arugula and duck salad with
mango, spiced pecans and, 188–189
Maui, and sweetbreads, grilled, baby turnip
greens with, 234–235
Maui, foie gras and pears, grilled, mesclun
with, 226–227
pickled, bitter greens with fried oysters, corn
and, 228–229
sweet-sour, and watermelon, watercress salad
with, 72–73
onions, red:
arugula with grilled vegetables and fresh
mozzarella, 254–255
Cary's leaf lettuce salad with orange, fennel
and, 56–57
grilled, arugula salad with dried tomatoes,
Parmesan and, 64–65
grilled, romaine and grilled salmon salad
with, 178–179 •
rings and new potatoes, lettuce of choice
with grilled, 74–75
oranges:
arugula and grapefruit salad, 62–63
Cary's leaf lettuce salad with fennel, red
onion and, 56–57
oysters, fried, bitter greens with corn, pickled
onion and, 228–229

Pancetta, 37
arugula with lobster and, 217
mesclun with roasted clams and, 144–145
P.L.T. salad with giant black olive croutons,
92–93
papayas, 38
escarole with fried plantains and, 194–195
and red snapper ceviche, arugula salad with,
132–133
in Yucatán cabbage salad, 212–213
Parmesan:
arugula salad with dried tomatoes, grilled red
onions and, 64–65
in regulation Caesar salad with lots of garlic
croutons, 58–59
in romaine lettuce with green beans, sausage
and peppers, 176–177•
in romaine salad with Gorgonzola, roasted
red peppers and polenta croutons, 232–233
in Southwestern Caesar salad, 60–61
in tomato and bread salad, 252–253
parsley, 19
and tomato salad with bulgur and feta
cheese, 83
peaches:
grilled, green leaf lettuce with blue cheese
and, 198–199
spinach salad with roast chicken and, 180–
181•
pearl onions, caramelized, arugula and duck
salad with mango and spiced pecans, 188–
189 •
pears:
and chicory salad, roasted, 66–67
foie gras and Maui onion, grilled, mesclun
with, 226–227

watercress and endive salad with blue cheese
and, 120–121
peas, Boston lettuce with poached salmon,
sweet potato and, 138–139 •
pea shoots, 29
pecans:
arugula and duck salad with mango,
caramelized onions and, 188–189 •
in salad of watercress, apple and ham, 131–
132
peppers, green bell:
leaf lettuce with grilled scallops, green olives
and, 174–175 •
romaine lettuce with green beans, sausage
and, 176–177 •
peppers, red bell:
arugula with grilled vegetables and fresh
mozzarella, 254–255
leaf lettuce with grilled scallops, green olives
and, 174–175 •
romaine lettuce with green beans, sausage
and, 176–177•
spinach salad with eggplant, roasted garlic
and, 114–115
peppers, roasted red bell, 42
Doctor Hibachi's spinach salad with grilled
lamb, garlic chips and, 152–153 •
romaine salad with Gorgonzola, polenta
croutons and, 232–233
pickles, chicory with garlic pork, black-eyed
peas and, 172–173 •
pineapple:
Bibb lettuce with grilled scallops, sausage
and, 224–225
Boston lettuce with grilled pork and, 192–
193
grilled, Tommy's red cabbage salad with,
248–249
spinach salad with grilled shrimp and, 154–
155
plantains, 38
fried, escarole with papayas and, 194–
195
P.L.T. salad with giant black olive croutons, 92–
93
plums, watercress salad with scallions and, 70–
71
polenta croutons, romaine salad with
Gorgonzola, roasted red peppers and,
232–233
pomegranate:
molasses, 38
seeds, romaine with turnips and, 206–
207
pork:
arugula with grilled prosciutto and figs, 242–
243
arugula with lobster and pancetta, 217
Boston lettuce with grilled pineapple and
pancetta, 192–193
garlic, chicory with pickles, black-eyed peas
and, 172–173 •
mesclun with roasted clams and, 144–145
P.L.T. salad with giant black olive croutons,
92–93

potatoes:
  Grandma Wetzler's escarole salad with
    bacon, eggs and, 54–55
  new, lettuce of choice with grilled red onion
    rings and, 74–75
  Red Bliss, in arugula with grilled vegetables
    and fresh mozzarella, 254–255
  spinach salad with mangoes and, 208–209
prosciutto, arugula with grilled figs and, 242–243
purslane, 32

quail:
  grilled, watercress and rice noodle salad with,
    166–167•
  pepper-crusted, arugula salad with
    pumpernickel croutons and, 164–165 •

radicchio, 18, 32
  and arugula with grilled mozzarella and
    bread skewers, 244–245
  bitter greens with fiery seared squid, 190–191
  watercress and endive with smoked salmon,
    150–151
  and watercress salad with beets and leeks,
    122–123
  weight of, 23
raisins:
  dark, in salad of watercress, apple and ham,
    131–132
  in frisée with apple, cucumber and walnuts,
    124–125
ribs, chef's salad with, 142–143
rice noodle and watercress salad with grilled
  quail, 166–167•
romaine, romaine salad, 18
  with buttermilk fried chicken livers, 230–231
  with crispy fried squid, 148–149
  with goat cheese and navy beans, 104–105
  with Gorgonzola, roasted red peppers and
    polenta croutons, 232–233
  with green apples and stuffed tortillas, 202–203
  with green beans, sausage and peppers, 176–
    177•
  and grilled eggplant with feta and green
    grapes, 250–251
  with grilled new potatoes and red onion
    rings, 74–75
  and grilled salmon salad with grilled red
    onions, 178–179 •
  hearts of, with roasted beets and asparagus,
    106–107
  regulation Caesar salad with lots of garlic
    croutons, 58–59
  Southwestern Caesar salad, 60–61
  tomato and avocado salad with cornbread
    croutons, 86–87
  and tortilla salad with avocado, 204–205
  with turnips and pomegranate seeds, 206–207
  weight of, 23

Salmon:
  poached, Boston lettuce with peas, sweet
    potato and, 138–139 •
  salad, grilled, romaine and, with grilled red
    onions, 178–179 •

salmon, smoked:
  watercress, endive and radicchio with, 150–
    151
  watercress with green grapes, hard-cooked
    egg and, 236–237
sauce, tidewater tartar, 162–163
sausage:
  Bibb lettuce with grilled scallops, pineapple
    and, 224–225
  romaine lettuce with green beans, peppers
    and, 176–177 •
scallions, watercress salad with plums and, 70–
  71
scallops:
  Bibb lettuce with grilled sausage, pineapple
    and, 224–225
  leaf lettuce with grilled peppers, green olives
    and, 174–175 •
sesame oil, 38
shiitake mushrooms, wilted spinach salad with
  bacon and, 222–223
shrimp:
  arugula salad with white beans and, 136–
    137
  poached, Bibb lettuce with avocado,
    cornbread croutons and, 168–169 •
  poached, mi•ed cabbage salad with hearts of
    palm and, 140–141
  spinach salad with grilled pineapple and,
    154–155
sirloin, seared, and arugula salad, 218–219 •
skewers:
  grilled lamb and apricot, spinach salad with,
    182–183 •
  grilled mozzarella and bread, arugula and
    radicchio with, 244–245
Smithfield ham, dandelion greens with
  nectarines and, 68–69
smoked salmon:
  green grapes, watercress with hard-cooked
    egg and, 236–237
  watercress, endive and radicchio with, 150–
    151
snapper, red, ceviche, arugula salad with
  papaya and, 132–133
softshell crabs, sautéed, arugula with toast
  points and, 162–163 •
Southeast Asian–style napa cabbage slaw, 126–
  127
Southwestern Caesar salad, 60–61
spinach, spinach salad, 17, 19, 32
  with grilled lamb, roasted peppers and garlic
    chips, Doctor Hibachi's, 152–153 •
  with grilled lamb and apricot skewers, 182–
    183 •
  with grilled shrimp and pineapple, 154–155
  and lentil salad with toasted walnuts, 116–117
  with mangoes and potato, 208–209
  with peppers, eggplant and roasted garlic,
    114–115
  with roast chicken and peaches, 180–181•
  with spicy yellow split peas, 118–119
  weight of, 23
  wilted, salad with shiitake mushrooms and
    bacon, 222–223

split peas, yellow, spinach salad with spicy, 118–119
squid:
  fiery seared, bitter greens with, 190–191
  romaine salad with crispy fried, 148–149
star anise, 39
steak, flank, chile-rubbed, spicy cabbage salad with, 170–171 •
summer vegetables, sweet and sour cabbage salad with, 241–242
sweetbreads, baby turnip greens with grilled Maui onion and, 234–235
sweet potatoes:
  Boston lettuce with poached salmon, peas and, 138–139 •
  chicory salad with bacon, lemon-flavored crumbs and, 146–147
  oak leaf lettuce with grilled asparagus and, 98–99
sweet and sour, sweet-sour:
  cabbage salad with summer vegetables, 241–242
  onion and watermelon, watercress salad with, 72–73

tamarind, 39
tangerines, red leaf lettuce with jicama and, 102–103
tartar sauce, tidewater, 162–163
tatsoi, 18, 29
  bitter greens with fiery seared squid, 190–191
toast points, arugula with sautéed softshell crabs and, 162–163 •
tomatoes:
  and bread salad, 252–253
  dried, arugula salad with grilled red onions, Parmesan and, 64–65
  fried green, arugula salad with, 112–113
  local salad Johnson, 50–51
  oven-dried, 41–42
  plum, in arugula and seared sirloin salad, 218–219
  plum, in arugula with grilled vegetables and fresh mozzarella, 254–255
  in Southwestern Caesar salad, 60–61
tomato salad:
  aromatic watercress, herb and, 90–91
  August tomato and basil salad, 81
  Boston lettuce with tomato and blue cheese, 82
  fancy greens with tomatoes and grilled garlic-herb bread, 84–85
  leaf lettuce with tomato, cucumber and feta, 88–89
  parsley and, with bulgur and feta cheese, 83
  P.L.T. salad with giant black olive croutons, 92–93
  romaine, avocado and, with cornbread croutons, 86–87
tortillas:
  and romaine salad with avocado, 204–205
  stuffed, romaine lettuce with green apples and, 202–203

tuna:
  #1, and mizuna with daikon, salad of, 200–201
  peppered, red leaf lettuce with, green beans, olives and, 160–161 •
turnip greens, 17
  baby, with grilled sweetbreads and Maui onion, 234–235
  salad of young cooking greens, 49
turnips, romaine with pomegranate seeds and, 206–207

vegetables:
  grilled, arugula with fresh mozzarella and, 254–255
  summer, sweet and sour cabbage salad with, 241–242
vinaigrette:
  barbecue, 142–143
  basil, 114–115, 136–137
  caper-fennel, 110–111
  chile, 196–197
  chunky roasted pepper, 242–243
  creamy chipotle, 86–87
  creamy garlic-lemon, 176–177
  Cumberland, 188–189
  curry-lime, 159–160
  ginger-lemongrass, 90–91
  ginger-soy, 126–127
  herb, 92–93
  ice cube, 241–242
  lime-chile, 190–191
  mustard-horseradish, 150–151
  Nick's, 97–98
  oil and balsamic vinegar, 81
  olive oil and lemon, 84
  romesco, 174–175
  shallot, 50–51
  sherry-herb, 220–221
  simple, 83
  simple balsamic, 82
  simple lemon, 62–63
  simple sherry, 76–77
  spicy balsamic, 74–75
  spicy cumin, 104–105
  tartar, 228–229
  very simple, 72–73
  see also dressing
vinegar, 39–40

walnuts, frisée with apple, cucumbers and, 124–125
wasabi, 40
watercress, 17, 18, 33
  apple and ham, salad of, 131–132
  bitter greens with fiery seared squid, 190–191
  endive and radicchio with smoked salmon, 150–151
  and endive salad with pears and blue cheese, 120–121
  with green grapes, smoked salmon and hard-cooked egg, 236–237
  and grilled chicken salad with mangoes and grapes, 159–160 •

watercress (*continued*)
   with poached mussels and asparagus, 210–211
   and radicchio salad with beets and leeks,
      122–123
   and rice noodle salad with grilled quail, 166–
      167 •
   salad with plums and scallions, 70–71•
   salad with watermelon and sweet-sour onion,
      72–73
   tomato and herb salad, aromatic, 90–91

   weight of, 23
watermelon, watercress salad with sweet-sour
   onion and, 72–73
white beans, arugula salad with shrimp and,
   136–137
wilted spinach salad with shiitake mushrooms
   and bacon, 222–223

Yucatán cabbage salad, 212–213